THE
Electric
Guitar

THE
Electric
Guitar

Nick Freeth & Charles Alexander

COURAGE
BOOKS

AN IMPRINT OF RUNNING PRESS
PHILADELPHIA • LONDON

Nick Freeth

Nick Freeth was born in London in 1956. After graduating from St. Catharine's College, Cambridge with a degree in English Literature, he joined the BBC in 1978, and later became a senior producer in the World Service, where he specialized in making radio programs covering folk, jazz, and blues. Nick left the BBC in 1990 to work as Senior Producer for the London radio station Jazz FM, producing the 26-part series "100 Years of Jazz" and a wide range of other shows. In 1992, he was appointed Head of Music Production at Rewind Productions, an independent company making radio programs for the BBC; his credits there included series presented by Maddy Prior of Steeleye Span, and country music star Emmylou Harris. In 1994, Nick and Charles Alexander formed their own production company, Gleneagle Productions, whose recent BBC radio commissions have included a 12-part survey of "The Guitar in Jazz," and a series examining the history of jazz in Nazi Germany. He is the author, with Charles Alexander, of *The Acoustic Guitar*.

Nick is a self-taught guitarist, who has performed in a number of amateur bands in the London area, and enjoys listening to good playing in many different styles. Among his favorite guitarists are Ry Cooder, Jerry Garcia, James Burton, and Derek Bailey.

Charles Alexander

An active jazz guitarist for over 30 years, Charles Alexander performs with several groups on the London jazz scene and is Jazz Guitar Tutor at Richmond Adult and Community College.

Born in Edinburgh, Scotland, Charles took up guitar at the age of 14, inspired by early rock 'n' roll, R & B, and the music of Django Reinhardt. He played his first gig at 15 on a Hofner bass guitar and later supplemented his student grant playing with local rock bands, dance bands, and jazz groups. In 1973 he moved to London to become Director of the Jazz Centre Society, a non-profitmaking organization that produced hundreds of jazz events ranging from weekly club gigs to full-scale festivals. From 1980 to 1988 he was President of the International Jazz Federation. In 1984 he founded Jazzwise Publications, which markets printed jazz music and study materials and organizes jazz courses, including the Jamey Aebersold Jazz Summer School. He is publisher of the monthly *Jazzwise* magazine.

As a radio broadcaster, Charles wrote and presented the 12-part series "The Guitar in Jazz" for BBC Radio 3 and presented seven series of "Six Silver Strings" programs for BBC Radio 2, featuring a wide range of guitar music. He is a partner with co-author Nick Freeth in the independent radio production company Gleneagle Productions. He is the author, with Nick Freeth, of *The Acoustic Guitar*.

PHOTOGRAPHERS
Neil Sutherland & Don Eiler

EDITOR
Philip de Ste. Croix

DESIGNER
Phil Clucas MSIAD

PUBLISHING DIRECTOR
Will Steeds

PRODUCTION
Neil Randles & Karen Staff

PRODUCTION DIRECTOR
Graeme Procter

COLOR REPRODUCTION
Global Colour Separation Ltd

PRINTED AND BOUND IN SINGAPORE
Star Standard Industries (Pte) Ltd

5127 The Electric Guitar

Created by Quadrillion Publishing Ltd,
Godalming, Surrey, England
Copyright ©1999 Quadrillion Publishing Ltd
First published in the United States in 1999 by
Running Press

9 8 7 6 5 4 3 2 1
Digit on the right indicates the number of this printing.

Library of Congress Cataloging-in-Publication Number 98-68519

ISBN 0-7624-0522-8

Published by Courage Books, an imprint of Running Press Book Publishers,
125 South Twenty-second Street, Philadelphia, Pennsylvania 19103-4399

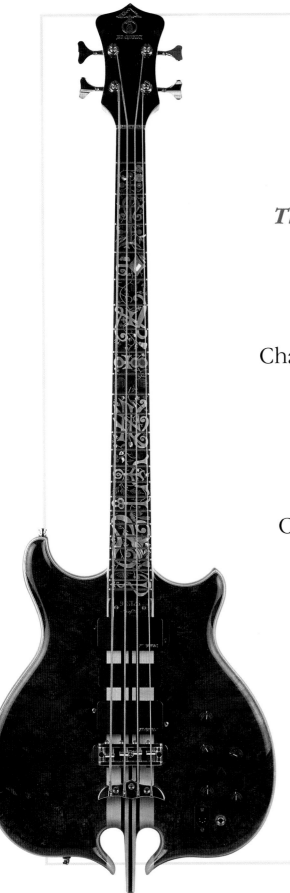

Contents

Acknowledgements

The authors would like to express their gratitude to the many guitar makers, players, dealers, collectors and museums who have assisted them in the preparation of this book. Especial thanks to Jonas Aronson and Benjamin Sitnikoff, Amanda's Texas Underground, Nashville; Geoff Beauchamp, Sales and Artist Liasion, EMI Guitar Division; Robyn Becker; Robert and Cindy Benedetto; Ed Bicknell; Simon Blundell, Sales Manager, Rose-Morris, London; Joshua Breakstone; Jimmy Bruno; Emmett and Yuta Chapman, Stick Enterprises, Inc.; Lloyd Chiate and Mikey Wright, Voltage Guitars, Hollywood; Chris Cobb, Ben Levin, Gary Brawer, and Heath Haberlin, Real Guitars, San Francisco; Stewart Cockett; Brenda Collady, Grand Ole Opry Museum, Nashville; Trevor Dean, Rosendean Fine Guitars; Paul Evans; Wally Evans and Graham Stockley, Barnes & Mullins Ltd; John Firth; Marie Gaines, McGregor Gaines, and Don Young, National Reso-Phonic Guitars; Peter Goalby and Trevor Wilkinson, Patrick Eggle Guitars; David Gilmour; Stephen Graham, editor of *Jazzwise* magazine; John C. Hall, Chairman & CEO, Rickenbacker International Corporation; Gary R. Hernandez, San Diego Guitars, Inc.; Jerry Jones, Jerry Jones Guitars, Nashville; Steve Klein and Lorenzo German, Klein Electric Guitars; Mark Knopfler; Robert Lane; Paul Leader; Mark Makin; Hugh Manson; John C. McLaren, Chairman, BBE Sound; Johnny McLaren, Plant Manager, G & L Musical Instruments; Mark Medley, Country Music Hall of Fame & Museum, Nashville; Rod Norwood and Hank Sable, Rod & Hank's Vintage Guitars, Inc., Memphis; Dave Peabody; John Peden; Rudy Pensa, Pensa Guitars, New York; Pete Strayer, Micky Butler, and Francis Johns, Gibson USA; Glenn Saggers; Eric Schoenberg; Jon Sievert; Stephen Strachan; Phil Taylor, DGM Music Ltd.; Doug Tulloch; Rick Turner, Rick Turner Guitars; Stan Werbin and Steve Szilagyi, Elderly Instruments, Lansing, Michigan; Ron, Susan and Mica Wickersham, Alembic, Inc.; Gary Wineroth and Doug Corrigan, Guitar Showcase, San Jose; Chris Winslet.

Our sincere thanks also to Neil Sutherland, who took the vast majority of the photographs for this book, and to the other two photographers who worked with us on the project: Don Eiler and John Alflatt.

The 1890 guitar patent, described on pages 14-15 and preserved in the Rickenbacker archives, was drawn to our attention by Mr. John C. Hall, Chairman & CEO of Rickenbacker International Corporation.

The quotations on pages 28-29, 80-81 and 108-109 are taken from Forrest White's book *Fender: The Inside Story* (© 1994 Forrest White), and are reproduced by kind permission of the copyright holder, and the publishers, GPI Books/Miller Freeman Books.

The quotations on pages 34-35 and 108-109 are taken from Richard R. Smith's book *Fender: The Sound Heard 'Round The World* (© 1995 Richard R. Smith), and are reproduced by kind permission of the copyright holder, and the publishers, Garfish Publishing Co.

The quotations from Ted McCarty on pages 54-55 and 84-85 are taken from *The Gibson* (© 1996 Rittor Music Europe Ltd./International Music Publications Ltd.) and are reproduced by kind permission of the copyright holders and publishers.

The quotations from Hank Garland on pages 62-63 are taken from his interview in the January 1981 issue of *Guitar Player* magazine (© 1981 Guitar Player), and are reproduced by kind permission of the copyright holder.

The quotations from Chet Atkins on pages 74-75 are taken from *The Gretsch Book* by Tony Bacon & Paul Day (© 1996 Tony Bacon & Paul Day), and are reproduced by kind permission of the copyright holders, and the publishers, Balafon Books.

The quotations from George Fullerton on pages 96-97 are taken from his interview with Willie G. Moseley in the October, November and December 1991 issues of *Vintage Guitar* magazine, as reprinted in *Stellas & Stratocasters* by Willie G. Moseley (© 1994 Willie G. Moseley), and are reproduced by kind permission of the copyright holder, and the publishers, Vintage Guitar Books.

The quotations from Robert Lane on pages 112-113 are taken from his website, http://www.jacksoncharvelworld.com/, and are reproduced by his kind permission.

The quotation from Stewart Cockett on pages 132-133 is taken from his article *Rosendean Handmade Guitars*, which first appeared on the Musicweb UK website (http://www.musicweb-uk.com/), and is reproduced by his kind permission.

Photograph by Deborah Feingold

Foreword by Mark Knopfler

Guitars happen for me even before girls do, but by the time I've got both of them shimmering in my head there's not much room left for anything else. I am toiling unwillingly to school in Newcastle dreaming of being in a beat group, although right now I haven't even got a guitar, never mind an amplifier.

My daily trudge is a mile or so but it is suddenly broken by the shocking presence of a Fender Stratocaster in the window of the little music shop at the bottom of Salters Road. It is the first one I've ever seen, Salmon Pink and priced at a truly monumental and impossible sum.

Every day I press up against the window to be as close to it as I can. I've already sent away for the catalogues and spend hours drooling over Fenders, Gibsons and Epiphones. I stand next to a boy making a Fender copy in the woodwork room just so I can get to pick up the body now and then and marvel at the shape and contours.

It takes years to get my hands on top-of-the-line instruments made in the classic years, but the plus side of all this is that I develop an affection for many of the cheaper makes: Futurama, early Burns, Watkins, Danelectro, Silvertone, Harmony, and my own beloved red Hofner, fifty quid and as near as my dad can reach to a Strat. I also learn to play and to love acoustic guitars of all shapes and sizes.

You'll have gathered by now that I was slightly obsessed, and I suppose I still am. A row of guitars in a window still pulls me over to the side of the road. I like to play guitars, to talk about them, to touch them and to look at them. I like to read about them too, and the story of the electric guitar is a fascinating one. You can read it here, and if you are even a little bit like me and you've got this fabulous book lying around you can simply indulge the look-and-linger habit to your heart's content. I'm still doing it.

Mark Knopfler
London, 1999

Introduction

After completing our previous book, *The Acoustic Guitar*, in 1998, it seemed logical to produce a sequel dealing with the electric instrument; but as we planned this new volume, it became clear that it would need to be structured rather differently. Acoustic guitars evolved over hundreds of years, but electrics, which made their first serious impact on the music scene as recently as the 1930s, have developed far more quickly. Only 20 years separate the first-ever mass-produced electric guitar, Electro's innovative but primitive "Frying Pan," from the Gibson Les Paul, a mature design that is still bought and used by thousands of today's players. And other comparatively early instruments, such as Fender's Telecaster and Stratocaster, have also shown remarkable staying power, surviving alongside newer models and retaining the loyalty and affection of countless musicians and audiences since their introduction in the 1950s.

Accordingly, after examining the early years of the electric guitar in Chapter 1, we devote an entire section of the book to these and other classic designs. While our focus is firmly on the market leaders in electric guitar manufacture, Fender and Gibson, we also include key models by other influential makers – and show how all the major companies strove to generate publicity and recognition for their guitars by seeking out leading jazz, country, and (increasingly) pop and rock players as endorsees.

The long post-war run of success enjoyed by Gibson and Fender was followed by a more unsettled climate from the mid-1960s onwards. In many ways this period, which is reflected in Section Three, was a fruitful one for guitar buyers. Those professionals who could afford it were commissioning fine custom instruments from small, independent makers and individual luthiers. Meanwhile, for the impecunious amateur and beginner, factories in the Far East were beginning to offer a bewildering range of guitars looking outwardly similar to "classic" Fenders and Gibsons. The quality of these "copies" has always been highly variable (as many buyers can testify!). Accordingly, they are not represented in detail in our selection of photographs: given the size of the subject, and the limited space available, we have preferred instead to feature a broader selection of original designs.

In the last two decades, there have been more and more of these to choose from, as we demonstrate in Sections Three and Four. The archtop guitar has undergone a resurgence on both sides of the Atlantic, and fine examples by master craftsmen such as Robert Benedetto are included here. We show solid-bodies from Steve Klein, Rick Turner, and Alembic: three Californian makers whose guitars make a bold visual impact to match their outstanding sound. The work of Hugh Manson and other top British luthiers is also documented; and in conclusion we look at one of the few entirely new fretted instruments to have successfully established itself since the advent of the electric guitar itself: Emmett Chapman's Stick.

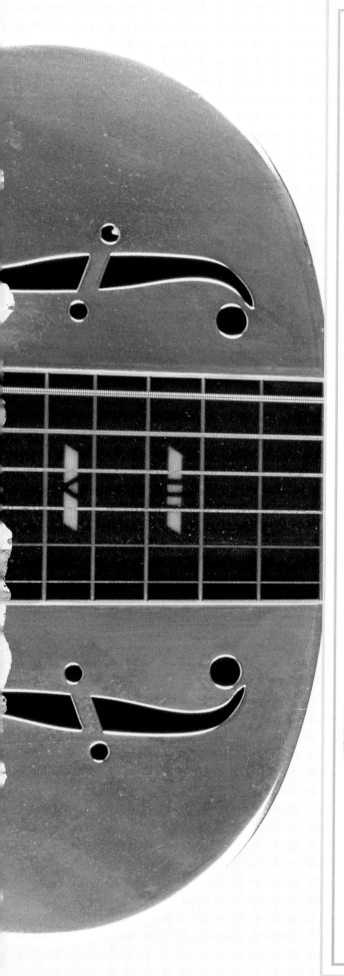

SECTION ONE:
The Birth of the Electric Guitar

The electric guitar evolved from theoretical concept to practical instrument in only a few decades. A wholly American creation, it was made possible by earlier developments in acoustic guitar design also pioneered in the New World. The most crucial of these was the introduction of steel strings on guitars by late nineteenth- and early twentieth-century luthiers. Steel was louder and more durable than the gut traditionally used on European-style classical instruments; but by the 1920s, American designers were starting to exploit the metal strings' magnetic characteristics as well as their acoustic properties. By mounting pickup systems near them and feeding the electrical signals created by their vibrations to amplifiers and loudspeakers, it was possible to produce a more powerful sound than even the biggest or most ingeniously designed acoustic instrument could create. In fact, a conventional, hollow wooden body was not strictly necessary at all – as George Beauchamp and Adolph Rickenbacker were soon to demonstrate with solid bodied guitars like the famous "Frying Pan."

Inevitably, the electric guitar generated a certain amount of initial resistance. Classical purists were quick to dismiss it as barbarous and offensive; and the great Spanish guitarist Andrés Segovia (1893–1987) allegedly branded it "an abomination." But as the 1930s progressed, a growing number of American players took up the amplified instrument. It gave them the opportunity to become true front-line soloists, trading licks with instruments that would once have overwhelmed them; and by the War years, the electric guitar had become widely accepted on the bandstand and in the recording studio.

Above: National "Silvo" electric lap steel, c.1937. The National String Instrument Corporation, founded in California in 1928, is most famous for its powerful-sounding acoustic resonator guitars. By the late 1930s, however, the company (which moved to Chicago in 1936) had responded to the growing demand for electric instruments with models like this one. It has a nickel-plated body and an "ebonoid" coverplate carrying its pickup assembly. Players with National acoustics could have their guitars converted to electric operation by having a similar "res-o-lectric" unit factory-fitted in place of the resonator. (Courtesy Mark Makin)

CHAPTER 1
THE EARLY YEARS
1930–1945

The electric guitar as we know it emerged during the 1930s, but the principles underlying its operation had been familiar to scientists since the previous century. Discoveries about the nature of electricity and magnetism made by Danish physicist Hans Oersted (1777–1851) and his great English contemporary, Michael Faraday (1791–1867) led to the development of the dynamo and other major technological breakthroughs. They also inspired a number of more eccentric inventions – such as the "apparatus for producing musical sounds by electricity," patented in 1890 by a U.S. naval officer, George Breed.

In his patent specification, Breed describes a method of using magnetism and battery power to create vibrations in wire strings, and explains how his ideas may be applied to the guitar and piano. Instruments using his system required extensive modifications. The guitar shown in the diagram opposite is fitted with a magnet, supported by a brace inside the body. Its strings pass between the poles of the magnet and across a metal bridge, which is wired to a rough-edged conducting wheel housed in a box at the tailpiece. This wheel, turned by a small clockwork motor, is connected, via a contact-spring, to a battery. The other side of the circuit comprises an electrical link between the battery and the instrument's frets, which are wired together.

When the player presses a string against a fret, the circuit is completed. A voltage from the battery passes to the contact-spring; the spinning conducting wheel, brushing against it, causes interruptions in the flow of electricity, creating a charge that is then introduced, via the bridge, into the magnetic field surrounding the strings. This makes the fretted string vibrate, sounding the selected note.

Breed's cumbersome, impractical guitar can have had little appeal to players, who would have been obliged to adapt their technique to master it, as no picking or strumming was possible. However, his instrument appears to be the first documented example of a guitar using electromagnetism, and some of its features – especially the "wrap-around" design for the string magnet – seem to anticipate the work of later pioneers like those discussed in the following pages.

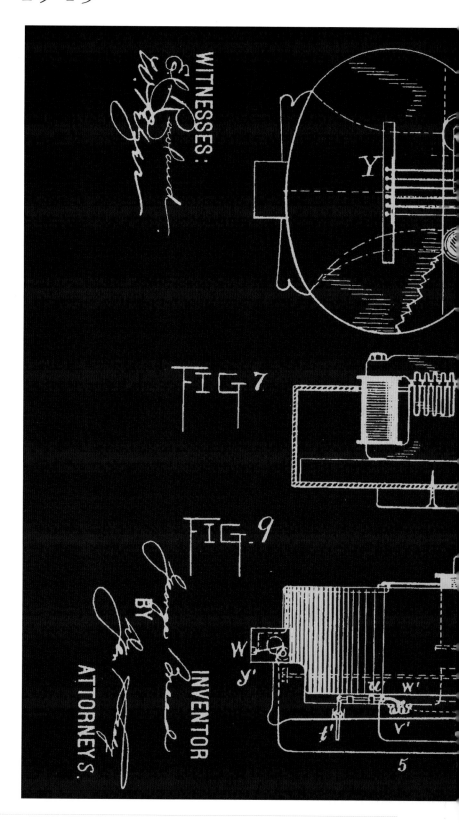

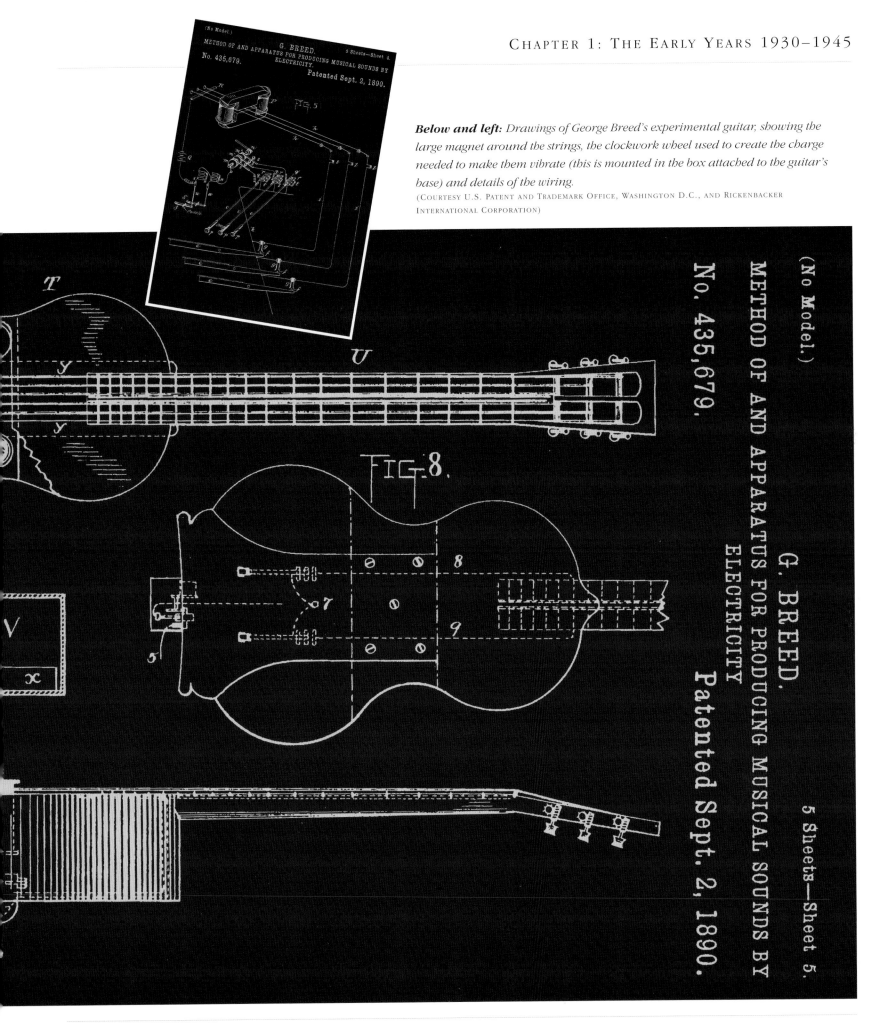

Below and left: Drawings of George Breed's experimental guitar, showing the large magnet around the strings, the clockwork wheel used to create the charge needed to make them vibrate (this is mounted in the box attached to the guitar's base) and details of the wiring.

George Beauchamp and the "Frying Pan"

The strings of George Breed's guitar were activated by electricity and magnetism, although the instrument still relied on a standard acoustic body to reflect and enhance its sound. But new technology soon opened up more radical possibilities. In 1907, Lee DeForest invented the triode, a vacuum tube capable of amplifying weak electrical signals, and this component, which provided an output strong enough to be fed to a loudspeaker, later became a key part of the circuitry used in radios and phonographs. The possibilities of electronic amplification also attracted the attention of guitar makers and players seeking to boost the volume of their instruments, and by the late 1920s, a few far-sighted designers were working on prototype guitars which were fitted with magnetic pickups, and intended to be connected to amplifier and speaker units.

Among them was George Beauchamp (d.1940), a vaudeville guitarist and co-founder of National Corporation, which was set up in California in 1928 to produce John Dopyera's tri-cone resonator guitars, the most powerful-sounding acoustics on the market. Beauchamp's time at National was stormy, and he was eventually ousted from the board of directors; but since well before his departure, he had been developing his own design for an electric guitar pickup. Its strings passed through two horseshoe-shaped magnets surrounding a coil wrapped around a core plate. The coil assembly was mounted below the strings, and when these were struck, they created a disturbance in the magnetic field around them; this was converted to a current by the coil and fed via an external amplifier to a loudspeaker.

This pickup became the basis for the first mass-produced electric guitar, a Hawaiian model nicknamed the "Frying Pan." To manufacture the instrument, Beauchamp and his supporters formed the Ro-Pat-In Corporation in 1931 (the company's odd name has never been explained). Based in Los Angeles, its directors included Beauchamp, Paul Barth (who collaborated on the pickup design), and Adolph Rickenbacker – a wealthy, innovative engineer who had manufactured steel bodies and resonators for National, and who was soon to play a crucial role in the subsequent development of the electric guitar industry.

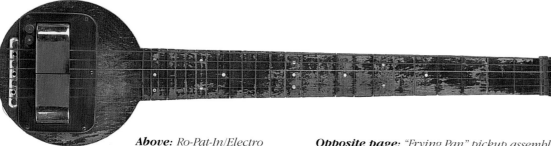

Above: *Ro-Pat-In/Electro "Frying Pan" Hawaiian guitar. This is the original prototype model, carved from a single piece of maple by an ex-National employee, Harry Watson (production "Frying Pans" were made of aluminum) and featuring George Beauchamp's innovative pickup design, for which he was granted a U.S. patent in 1937.*

(COURTESY RICKENBACKER INTERNATIONAL CORPORATION)

Opposite page: *"Frying Pan" pickup assembly. This close-up shows the pickup unit's massive steel horseshoe magnets, as well as the guitar's bridge and (beneath the left-hand magnet) the two screw terminals for the amplifier lead. Later models were fitted with a conventional jack socket.*

Right: *The "Frying Pan's" headstock shows no company name or decal. Some early production models had "Electro" engraved on them, and later, the familiar "Rickenbacher Electro" nameplate (see pages 22-23) was used.*

(COURTESY RICKENBACKER INTERNATIONAL CORPORATION)

Lloyd Loar and Vivi-Tone

R o-Pat-In's early models sold slowly, and for some time, other makers remained skeptical about the potential demand for electric instruments. Such conservative attitudes were understandable, particularly at companies such as Gibson, that already had extensive, successful ranges of fretted instruments, and were reluctant to devote time and money to what many players and luthiers still regarded as a gimmick.

However, not everyone at Gibson shared this cautious attitude. Lloyd Loar (1886–1943) had come to work at the firm's headquarters in Kalamazoo, Michigan, in 1919, and was responsible for the design of its highly acclaimed L-5 archtop acoustic guitar, which was launched in 1922. Subsequently, Loar turned his attention to amplified instruments, developing an electric viola and an electric bass in his workshop at Gibson. Unfortunately, the company's management decided not to market them, and in 1924 Loar resigned to pursue his ideas by himself. He eventually set up the Vivi-Tone Company in 1933, making guitars, mandolins, and (later) an electric keyboard –

Below: Vivi-Tone guitar, 1933. This design, made by musician, engineer, university teacher and former Gibson designer Lloyd Loar, was in production for little more than a year. Its innovative features (including the unusual pickup assembly mounted beneath the bridge) were patented by Loar in 1934.

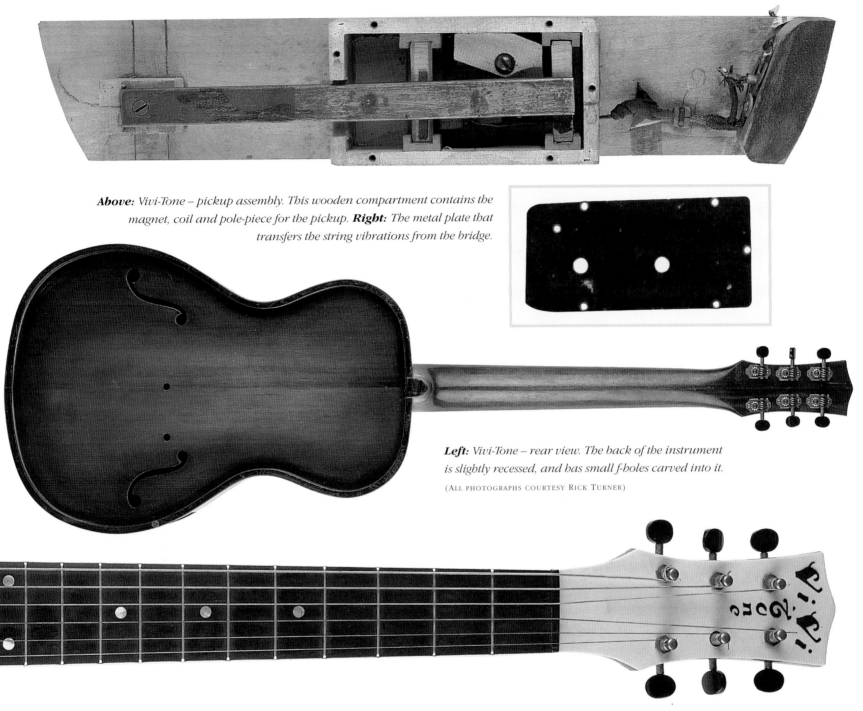

Above: *Vivi-Tone – pickup assembly. This wooden compartment contains the magnet, coil and pole-piece for the pickup.* **Right:** *The metal plate that transfers the string vibrations from the bridge.*

Left: *Vivi-Tone – rear view. The back of the instrument is slightly recessed, and has small f-holes carved into it.*

(ALL PHOTOGRAPHS COURTESY RICK TURNER)

although his designs brought him little commercial success.

The Vivi-Tone guitar shown here was presented by Loar to his friend Carl Christiansen, and has several remarkable features. The vibrations of its strings are passed from the bridge, via two steel screws, to a steel plate (clamped at one end and floating at the other) with a magnetic pickup mounted below it in a drawer-like compartment. The top of the guitar has no sound-holes, but its back has small f-holes, and is recessed about half an inch (1.27cm) into the body. American luthier Rick Turner, who owns the instrument, explains that Loar thought of the back as a secondary soundboard – an idea that is currently in favor with a number of modern classical guitar makers. Having played the Vivi-Tone through an amplifier, Rick says that its sound is disappointing, although this may be due to deterioration of some of the internal rubber parts. He suggests that renewing these might be "like putting fresh tires on an old Jaguar," and adds that restoring the guitar could make a great retirement project for him!

Gibson's First Electric Guitars

*I*n the 1920s, Gibson had ignored Lloyd Loar's urgings to introduce electric instruments, and it delayed its entry into the new market until 1936 – 12 years after his departure from the company. Gibson's first electric guitar was a Hawaiian model, the EH-150, which sold for $150 including a matching amplifier, and appeared that January. A few months later Gibson announced an archtop "Electric Spanish" guitar with the same serial number: the ES-150.

By the mid-1930s, Gibson's most popular acoustic archtops (including the L-5, L-7, and L-12) all had 17-inch (43.2cm) bodies, and in 1934 the company had brought out its top-of-the-range Super 400, which was 18 inches (45.7cm) wide. At just over 16 inches (40.6cm), the new ES-150 is more modestly sized, and altogether less visually striking than its more finely finished acoustic counterparts. Perhaps its most remarkable feature is its pickup, an ingenious design by Gibson's Walter Fuller: the unit's bulky magnets are hidden

Below: Gibson ES-150, 1937. The ES-150's top, fitted with X-braces, like the guitars in Gibson's acoustic archtop range, is made from spruce; the back and sides are maple.

beneath the guitar's spruce top, leaving only the blade-shaped polepiece, the coil cover, and the three mounting and adjusting screws visible. The instrument "plugs in" unobtrusively via a jack socket mounted in the tailpiece.

The ES-150 and its pickup are most closely associated with the brilliant jazzman Charlie Christian (1916–1942), whose interest in electric guitars was kindled when he met Eddie Durham (1906–1987) – probably the first major jazz player to use an amplified guitar on stage and on record – in the mid-1930s. Soon afterwards, Christian acquired one of the new Gibson models, and in 1939, he shot to fame as a member of the Benny Goodman band, where he pioneered the single-string, saxophone-like soloing style that helped to establish the electric guitar as a front-line jazz instrument. His high-profile use of the ES-150 influenced many other important artists – including his friend and sometime pupil T-Bone Walker (1910–1975) – to play it.

Gibson responded to the success of its first electric archtop by introducing a more finely decorated, 17-inch model, the ES-250, in 1939; this too was used and endorsed by Charlie Christian. Another new guitar, the ES-300, with its distinctive slanting pickup, appeared a year later, and is shown opposite.

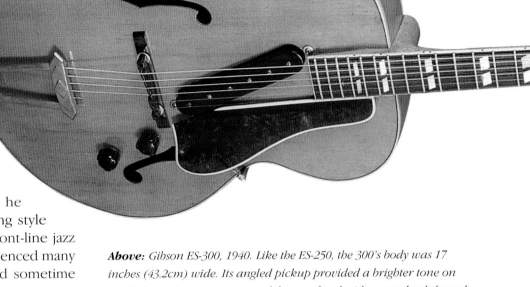

Above: *Gibson ES-300, 1940. Like the ES-250, the 300's body was 17 inches (43.2cm) wide. Its angled pickup provided a brighter tone on the higher strings; post-war models were fitted with a standard-shaped transducer. The instrument's finish, with double parallelogram fingerboard inlays, and a headstock decorated with a crown (soon to become a familiar feature on later Gibson models), was considerably more elaborate than the cheaper ES-150's.*

(COURTESY ELDERLY INSTRUMENTS: PHOTOGRAPH BY DAVE MATCHETTE)

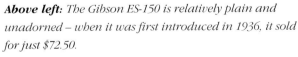

Above left: *The Gibson ES-150 is relatively plain and unadorned – when it was first introduced in 1936, it sold for just $72.50.*

(COURTESY LLOYD CHIATE, VOLTAGE GUITARS, HOLLYWOOD)

Left: *Charlie Christian playing his Gibson ES-150. On the right is the great jazz drummer Gene Krupa (1909–1973), also a member of the Benny Goodman band during the 1930s.*

(COURTESY CHRISTIAN HIM'S JAZZ INDEX PHOTO LIBRARY)

Electro:
The Pre-War Years

Ro-Pat-In launched its aluminum "Frying Pan" Hawaiian guitar in 1932; later the same year, it brought out a wooden-bodied "Spanish" model that also used George Beauchamp's "horseshoe" pickup. Both guitars appeared under the "Electro" brand name; in 1934, Beauchamp, Adolph Rickenbacker, and Paul Barth rechristened their company the Electro String Instrument Corporation, and added the Rickenbacker name (mis-spelt as "Rickenbacher" – see caption below) to their headstock decals.

For the rest of the decade, Electro continued to develop and innovate, introducing Hawaiian and Spanish guitars made of Bakelite, combo amplifiers, and some strikingly futuristic electric violins and basses constructed using plastics and aluminum. The company's wooden instruments often had bodies sourced from other manufacturers. The Harmony Company of Chicago built the body for the original 1932 Electro Spanish, and the guitar shown opposite, a rare instrument without a serial number dating from 1937, has a body made by Kay.

The manufacture of products such as the Bakelite lapsteel (also illustrated here) drew on Adolph Rickenbacker's prodigious engineering skills. For a while, he had worked alongside the Belgian-born inventor of Bakelite, L.H. Baekeland (1863–1944); and his later industrial experience included a spell at Hotpoint, where he pioneered advanced injection molding techniques, solving the long-standing problem of sticking and breakage within the mold by the addition of a well-known brand of scouring powder to the plastic mix! John C. Hall, Rickenbacker's present Chairman and CEO, acknowledges the importance of Adolph's technical ability to Electro's success: "If you look back at [his] use of materials, it's quite extraordinary what he achieved." However, Mr. Hall believes that ultimately, the founder's greatest contribution to his firm was probably financial: "He was a pretty wealthy guy, and more than anything, it was his cash that kept National and later Rickenbacker going."

In 1940, George Beauchamp resigned from Electro due to ill health, and died later that year. Adolph Rickenbacker maintained the company's instrument production until 1942, when the Electro factory was obliged to take up war-related work; but in the post-war years, the company would soon resume its major role on the guitar scene.

Above: *The spelling of "Rickenbacher" (with an "h") on the decal is a misprint that appears on a number of other guitars and amps made by the company from the 1930s until the early 1950s – but not on its printed publicity material. Adolph Rickenbacker anglicized the spelling of his name before 1920, and always signed it with a "k" thereafter.*
Left: *Rickenbacker combo amplifier, 1930s. Early models like these were often sold with a specific instrument as a "set."*

(COURTESY RICKENBACKER INTERNATIONAL CORPORATION)

Left: *Rickenbacker archtop, 1937. Only two examples of this model exist at Rickenbacker's headquarters in Santa Ana: this instrument has a body by the Chicago guitar-maker Kay, and the other guitar's body was built by Harmony. Both feature the same distinctive Beauchamp-style pickup assembly.*
(COURTESY RICKENBACKER INTERNATIONAL CORPORATION)

Above: *Rickenbacker lap-steel, pre-World War II. This chrome-decorated Bakelite Hawaiian guitar has undergone some modifications (including the addition of a Vibrola vibrato unit), but its pre-war status is confirmed by the 1 1/2-inch (3.8cm) width of its pickup magnet. When large-scale production of Rickenbackers resumed in 1946, the size of their magnets was reduced to 1 1/4 inches (3.2cm). The company also produced seven-, eight- and ten-string lap steels, as well as double-neck models.*
(COURTESY ELDERLY INSTRUMENTS: PHOTOGRAPH BY DAVE MATCHETTE)

23

SECTION TWO:
The Classic Designs

During the war years, the manufacture of "non-essential" goods was strictly limited, and American instrument makers were obliged to focus much of their energy and manpower on defense-related work. With the end of hostilities, guitar production was scaled up again, but it soon became clear that the market had changed. Demand for electric instruments was outstripping acoustic sales, and long-established companies such as Gibson – whose output in the immediate post-war years was still dominated by labor- and cost-intensive acoustic archtop models – had to adapt quickly to the new situation. Significantly, one of the first innovations introduced by the firm's new General Manager (later its President), Ted McCarty (b.1909), when he took over in 1948, was the introduction of a detachable pickup unit that could "electrify" archtops without extensive modification. Later, McCarty was to preside over Gibson's "golden years" of modernization and expansion – as well as supervising the introduction of its most famous solid-body model, the Les Paul, in 1952.

By contrast, former radio repair man Leo Fender (1909–1991) and his small, California-based company, were relative newcomers to guitar manufacture. Leo himself was not a "traditional" luthier, but a skilled engineer with a firm grounding in practical electronics. His basic, functional solid-body instruments were easy to mass-produce and maintain, with pickup assemblies that simply slotted into place, and necks that could be removed by unscrewing just four bolts. The Fender Telecaster (1950) and Stratocaster (1954) rapidly became accepted as classics, and are perhaps the most profoundly influential of all electric guitar designs.

While Fender and Gibson set the pace for the industry throughout the 1950s and early 1960s, a considerable number of other makers were also catering for the electric guitar boom. This section features a broad cross-section of their instruments, from the exclusive Gretsch White Falcon, with its gold-leaf finish and $600 price tag, to the inexpensive but brilliantly designed hardboard-bodied guitars of Nathan Daniel.

Gibson Les Paul Standard, 1958. An early example of this classic model, dating from the year of its introduction. Pre-1960 Standards are among the most desirable and valuable of all Gibson solid electrics.

(COURTESY MARK KNOPFLER)

CHAPTER 2
THE SOLID-BODY ELECTRIC
1946–1965

(PHOTOGRAPH COURTESY
JON SIEVERT, SAN
FRANCISCO)

*I*n the post-war years, California retained its pre-eminence as a center for electric guitar development. In fact, a number of the main figures in the evolution of the instrument were friends, associates or rivals living within a few miles of the town of Fullerton, just east of Los Angeles. Its residents included Clayton O. Kauffman (known as "Doc"), who developed the Vibrola vibrato unit used on many Rickenbacker guitars; during the mid-1940s, Kauffman had a brief business partnership with Leo Fender, making instruments and amplifiers under the K & F brand name at Fender's radio shop in downtown Fullerton. Later, Fender amps and guitars were distributed by F.C. Hall, a businessman and engineer based in nearby Santa Ana. In 1953, Hall bought Adolph Rickenbacker's Electro String Company, re-named it after its founder, and played a central role in its subsequent international success.

A short distance away, in the Los Angeles suburb of Downey, lived Paul Bigsby, a guitar builder, repairer and machinist who was also an expert on motorcycles. It was probably a mutual enthusiasm for bikes that led to his friendship with the famous country guitar player Merle Travis (1917–1983), who had settled in Los Angeles after the war, and was working with Western Swing bands fronted by Cliffie Stone and Ray Whitley. In 1948, Travis commissioned a solid-bodied electric from Bigsby, and the resultant instrument had several unusual features. All six tuning machines were fitted onto one side of a distinctively carved headstock, and the neck was not glued or bolted at the heel, but extended right through the maple body, whose elegant single cutaway and striking finish made the "Travis-Bigsby" a guitar to remember.

Merle Travis subsequently claimed that the instrument caught Leo Fender's eye at a Cliffie Stone concert in Placentia (only a few miles from Fullerton), that Fender was allowed to borrow it, and that key aspects of its design were later incorporated into Fender's own guitars. Fender denied ever borrowing the Travis-Bigsby, and although the instrument has a few superficial similarities with his famous later models, it seems unlikely that it especially influenced him.

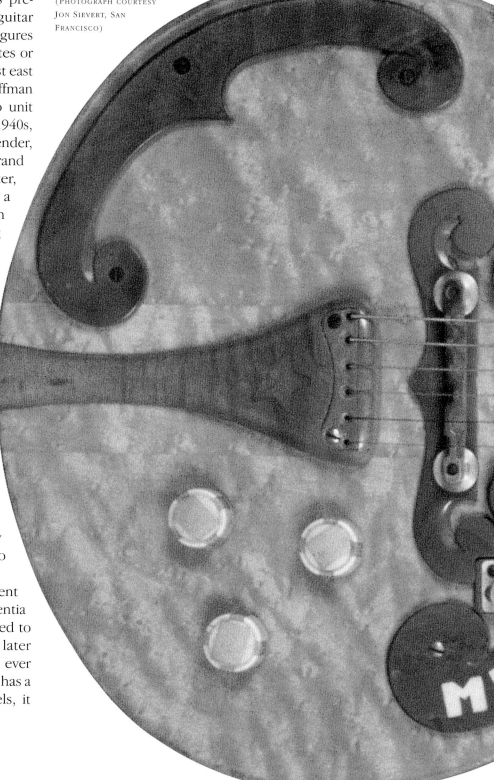

Left: *Travis-Bigsby solid electric guitar, 1948. The single-cutaway body is made from bird's-eye maple, with a polished walnut pickguard, bridge surround and tailpiece. The fingerboard has playing card symbol inlays. The shape of the headstock (**top of page**) and the positioning of the tuning machines, are two of the major similarities between the Travis-Bigsby and Leo Fender's guitars. However, such designs were in use in Europe over a century earlier, and are also found on some of the first acoustics made by the Martin company in Nazareth, Pennsylvania. Paul Bigsby later became famous for creating the guitar vibrato that bears his name.*

Leo Fender's Early Designs

Leo Fender made his first guitar in 1943, when he and Doc Kauffman collaborated on a crude instrument built from a single block of wood with a bought-in fingerboard attached. It was used as a test-bed for a prototype pickup the two men had developed – a design in which the strings pass through the device's coil, not over it as in conventional designs. This "Direct Sound" pickup subsequently featured on Leo and Doc's "K & F" lap steels, which went into production in 1945. By early 1946, their fledgling company was making about 40 instruments a week, often sold as "sets" with matching K & F amplifiers.

It was at this stage that Fender and Kauffman attracted the attention of Don Randall, the manager of a Santa Ana-based electronic component distribution company, Radio-Tel, owned by local businessman F.C. Hall (see earlier, page 26). Randall saw considerable potential in K & F, and persuaded his boss to offer them an exclusive distribution deal. Inevitably,

this would have involved the two guitar-makers in considerable expansion; but while Leo Fender was excited by the prospect, Doc Kauffman did not share his enthusiasm. According to one of Fender's closest associates, Forrest White, in his book *Fender: The Inside Story*, "Doc was apprehensive about investing more money in this as yet unproven venture. Leo said, 'Doc was scared because had a little real estate in Oklahoma which he didn't want to lose, so rather than take the risk, he left.'" However, the dissolution of the K & F partnership was an amicable one, and Leo Fender and Doc Kauffman remained close friends until Doc's death in 1990.

Leo went ahead with the Radio-Tel venture, setting up the Fender Electric Instrument Company in 1946, and developing and manufacturing an extensive range of lap steels and amplifiers over the next few years. But despite the sales deal, his firm had serious financial difficulties. It took the introduction of a revolutionary new product – Leo's mass-produced, solid electric guitar, designed, unlike his lap steels, for the regular "Spanish-style" player – to ensure Fender's survival, as well as its place in history.

Left: Fender Champion 600 combo amplifier, c.1949. This was the smallest amplifier in the Fender range, fitted with a single 6-inch (15.2cm) loudspeaker, and designed for student or practice use. The Champion 600 was introduced in 1949 as a companion to Fender's "Champion" range of lap steels, and renamed "Champ" in the early 1950s. The example shown here has lost its leather carrying handle, but is still in full working order after 50 years – a tribute to the "extremely rugged construction" mentioned in the original publicity for the amp. (COURTESY REAL GUITARS, SAN FRANCISCO)

These pages: *Leo Fender/Doc Kauffman prototype guitar, 1943. Despite its shape, this is actually a standard "Spanish-style" guitar, not a lap steel. According to Leo Fender, it was hired out to various musicians for concerts during the 1940s – although it cannot have been very easy or comfortable to play.*

*The prototype of 1943 is fitted with a Fender/Kauffman "Direct Sound" pickup (patented in 1948), whose volume and tone control wheels are visible **(left)** on either side of the strings. Leo Fender presented the guitar to the Roy Acuff Museum in Nashville, Tennessee in 1965.*

(PHOTOGRAPH COURTESY JOHN PEDEN, NEW YORK)

From "Standard Electric" to Telecaster

Unlike previous solid wood "electric Spanish" models, the guitar that Fender began to develop in 1949 was specifically conceived as a factory-made instrument, and intended to be as cheap and easy as possible to manufacture and repair. It had a basic, single-cutaway body shape and a bolted-on, detachable neck, as well as two important innovations: a new pickup with individual pole-pieces for each string, and an adjustable bridge to ensure better intonation.

By the end of 1949 two prototypes of the "Standard Electric," as the instrument was initially known, had been made; it was only on the second of these that Leo introduced his soon-to-be famous headstock with all six tuning machines on one side. In Spring 1950, the new model was formally announced by Fender and Radio-Tel; it was renamed the Esquire, and displayed for the first time at that year's National Association of Music Merchants (NAMM) show in Chicago.

Many of the earliest Esquires shown to dealers during the following weeks had warped necks, and Don Randall of Radio-Tel urged Fender to remedy this defect by installing metal truss-rods on the instruments. Meanwhile, Leo himself was planning a more fundamental change: the addition of a second pickup, fitted in the neck position. This was incorporated, along with the truss-rod, on the first production run of his new guitar in late 1950.

The extra pickup caused some concern among the sales force, which had been promoting a single-pickup instrument. The solution was to rename the modified two-pickup guitar the Broadcaster (although a number of two-pickup Esquires were also sold) and to delay the introduction of the single-pickup Esquire until the following year. Another snag also befell the new model; in February 1951, the New York-based Gretsch Company complained that the "Broadcaster" name infringed the "Broadkaster" trademark used on Gretsch's drumkits and banjos. Fender's initial response was to remove the word "Broadcaster" from its headstocks, but soon afterwards, it came up with yet another name for its two-pickup electric Spanish guitar: the Telecaster.

Above: Fender Broadcaster, c.1950. This instrument (serial number 0053) was made between the end of 1950 and February 1951, when an accusation of trademark violation from Gretsch forced Fender to change the name of its new model. It is owned by David Gilmour of Pink Floyd.

Below: Like the other guitars on these two pages, the Fender Broadcaster has an ash body, and a maple neck with a truss-rod fitted. The bridge allows pairs of strings to be adjusted for length and height, and the nearby "back" pickup (angled to give a cutting treble tone while also preserving lower-frequency response) can be raised and lowered to optimize its output level and sound. The Broadcaster was introduced at a retail price of $169.95.

(COURTESY DAVID GILMOUR)

Opposite page, left: Fender "No-caster," 1951. For a short period between Gretsch's complaint and the decision to rechristen its new guitar "Telecaster," Fender simply removed the word "Broadcaster" from the headstock decals (see inset on opposite page) – hence the curious nickname for this model. There are few other significant differences between "No-casters" and Broadcasters. On this example, the bridge/pickup assembly is fitted with a removable metal cover; an accessory (also supplied with later Telecasters) designed to shield the pickup from interference and damage. Most guitarists find it inhibits their playing, and either discard it or use it as an ashtray!

(COURTESY LLOYD CHIATE, VOLTAGE GUITARS, HOLLYWOOD)

Far right: *Fender Telecaster, 1952. By 1952, the Telecaster, now selling at $189.50, was becoming an increasingly familiar sight on bandstands throughout the USA. The previous year, Leo Fender had been granted a patent for his revolutionary design. The "butterscotch" finish and black pickguard seen on all the instruments shown here were the only standard color schemes initially available.*
(COURTESY GUITAR SHOWCASE, SAN JOSE)

Inset, left: *Two near-identical headstocks – the Fender No-Caster and the Fender Telecaster – show the omission that earned the former its nickname.*

The "Pre-CBS" Telecaster

The Fender Telecaster is a classic design, which has inspired and delighted guitar players for decades. Its appearance and shape have altered relatively little since its introduction – although more fundamental modifications have been made to its internal circuitry. These began as early as 1952, when Leo Fender made an important change to the pickup wiring.

Fender targetted the Broadcaster/Telecaster at the busy professional player of the early 1950s, who would want to take solos, provide rhythm accompaniment, and sometimes even pick out bass lines on his instrument. Accordingly, the original Tele offered three basic sounds, selected by the switch on the right of the strings: a "rhythm guitar" tone from the neck (or "front") pickup; a bassy timbre created by passing the front pickup signal through a special pre-set circuit; and a harder, more cutting "lead" tone from the back (bridge) pickup, which could be blended with the front pickup by adjusting the lower of the instrument's two knobs (the upper one is a volume control). The 1952 modification removed the "blend" function, substituting a conventional tone control. This meant that players could no longer combine the front and back pickups, and it was not until 1967 that the instrument was reconfigured in its "modern" form, offering a choice of front, back, or front and back pickups.

Below left: *Fender Telecaster, 1959. This guitar is finished in fiesta red – one of the "custom colors" offered by Fender to Telecaster purchasers. Bright, primary colors were not initially very popular, but soon caught on in the 1960s.*

By the time of the CBS takeover, possible options included foam green, candy apple red and daphne blue, as well as sunburst, black, and the original blond. (COURTESY SAN DIEGO GUITARS)

Below left: *Fender Telecaster, 1965. Leo Fender sold his company to CBS in January 1965, but it was some time before the new owners made any changes to the design of their products. This superb 1965 guitar has the same overall specification as a "pre-CBS" instrument.*
(COURTESY LLOYD CHIATE, VOLTAGE GUITARS, HOLLYWOOD)

At this time, the "bassy" circuit was finally abandoned; thanks to the popularity of the bass guitar – another Fender invention – it had become an anachronism.

Between 1951 and 1965 (the date when Leo Fender sold his company to CBS; see later, pages 78-79) several changes were made to the Telecaster's neck shape, and in 1959 the original all-maple neck was replaced by one with a rosewood fingerboard. There were also cosmetic changes to the instrument; a white pickguard was introduced in 1954, and soon afterwards, alternative body finishes began to be offered (at a five percent surcharge) – at first in any color of the player's choice, and later, in a range of specified "custom colors." A mahogany-bodied Telecaster was introduced in 1963, but discontinued two years later.

Above left: *Fender Telecaster, 1954. This example was one of the last 1954 Telecasters to be fitted with a black pickguard. Despite the launch of Fender's three-pickup Stratocaster in Spring '54, Tele sales continued to flourish; the following year, the company's Head of Sales, Don Randall, commented in* Down Beat *magazine that "Fender is having a hard time keeping up with demand for electric guitars".*
(COURTESY MARK KNOPFLER)

The Stratocaster –
Another First for Fender

*L*eo Fender was not a man to rest on his laurels, and after launching the Telecaster and Esquire, he quickly turned his attention to new projects. His groundbreaking Precision Bass Guitar appeared in 1951, and his next "electric Spanish" design, the Fender Stratocaster, has proved to be one of the most innovative (and widely copied) instruments of all time.

The "Stratocaster" name, with its image of high-flying modernity, was probably coined by Don Randall, previously General Manager at Radio-Tel, and then President of Fender Sales Inc., which took over distribution of Fender products in 1953. As Randall explains in Richard R. Smith's book *Fender: The Sound Heard 'Round the World,* "The Stratocaster's introduction was market driven. And without minimising Leo's invention, it was a composite of ideas from many players." Customer feedback from Telecaster owners had revealed some areas of dissatisfaction, especially with the instrument's body, which some of them found bulky and awkward. Meanwhile, other manufacturers were busily introducing rival solid guitars, and Fender needed an innovative new model of its own.

The response from Leo and his team was to create a radically different double cutaway shape for the Stratocaster, with "comfort contouring" on the back and at the point where the player rests his or her picking arm. The "Strat" would also have three pickups, and a patented vibrato system ("tremolo" in Fender nomenclature) combined with an innovative bridge setup allowing all six strings to be adjusted separately for length and height. (This addressed another weakness in the Telecaster, whose double bridge saddles did not permit precise intonation.) Among the Fender staffers who contributed to the design were Freddie Tavares, a skilled musician and craftsman who joined Fender in 1953, and George Fullerton, who had worked with Leo since 1948, and subsequently became his business partner and one of his closest friends.

The Stratocaster was introduced in 1954 with a fanfare of publicity, proclaiming it "years ahead in design – unequalled in performance." This judgment would quickly be echoed by its first players, including leading names from country music, blues and – a little later – rock and roll.

Below left and left: *Fender Stratocaster, 1954. This beautifully preserved instrument, nicknamed the "Jurassic Strat" by its owner, Mark Knopfler, dates from the year the model was introduced. Its body is made of ash, and it has a maple neck. The finish is "two-tone sunburst," which was supplied as standard until 1958, although various other colors were available at extra cost.*

(COURTESY MARK KNOPFLER)

Bottom right: *Fender Stratocaster, 1957. In 1956, according to guitar expert A.R. Duchossoir, Fender started using alder instead of ash for Stratocaster bodies, although no changes were made to their size or contours. The model shown here has its rarely seen metal bridge cover attached. The Strat's "synchronized tremolo" bridge was a major selling point; however, not all players favor vibratos, and the unit's controlling arm can easily be unscrewed and removed, as it has been here.*

(COURTESY ROOM 335, ROSE-MORRIS, LONDON)

The "Pre-CBS" Stratocaster

The first Stratocasters were sold for $249.50 (with tremolo) and $229.50 (without it). Like the Telecaster, the original Strat had an ash body and an all-maple neck; this was replaced in 1959 by a maple model with a rosewood fingerboard. The guitar was given a sunburst finish as standard, with custom colors, and eventually a range of Fender's "standardized" optional finishes, available at extra cost. In 1957, a deluxe Strat with gold-plated hardware was launched; confusingly, this good-looking model had a "Blond" finish of the kind that was standard on the Telecaster and Esquire.

Fender's "years ahead in design" claim for the Strat was certainly justified; in fact, some of the instrument's musical possibilities were not fully exploited until over a decade after its appearance. The tremolo/bridge unit, developed especially for the guitar and patented by Leo Fender in 1956, was able to produce much more dramatic effects than the gentle pitch fluctuations favored by most early Strat players. Unlike some other vibratos, it was able to keep the strings fairly well in tune after being used, and this encouraged a more extreme use of its capabilities by 1960s and '70s musicians, notably Jimi Hendrix.

There was also more to the Strat's electronics than may have been intended by its designer. The pickups were selected by a three-position switch, below which were three knobs: an overall volume control, and individual tone controls for the neck and middle pickup. (The bridge pickup was wired straight to the volume knob.) When the switch was used in its three standard settings, only one pickup at a time could be activated; but guitarists soon learned how to balance it between these positions to give combinations of neck-and-middle and middle-and-bridge pickups, creating unexpected and distinctive tone-colors. Surprisingly, it was many years before Fender fitted a five-position switch to make these sounds easier to obtain.

Stratocaster sales took a brief downturn in the early 1960s, but the instrument's longer-term popularity was unaffected. Today its only serious rival as the most sought-after of all solid electric guitars is the Gibson Les Paul, the origins and development of which are featured on the following pages.

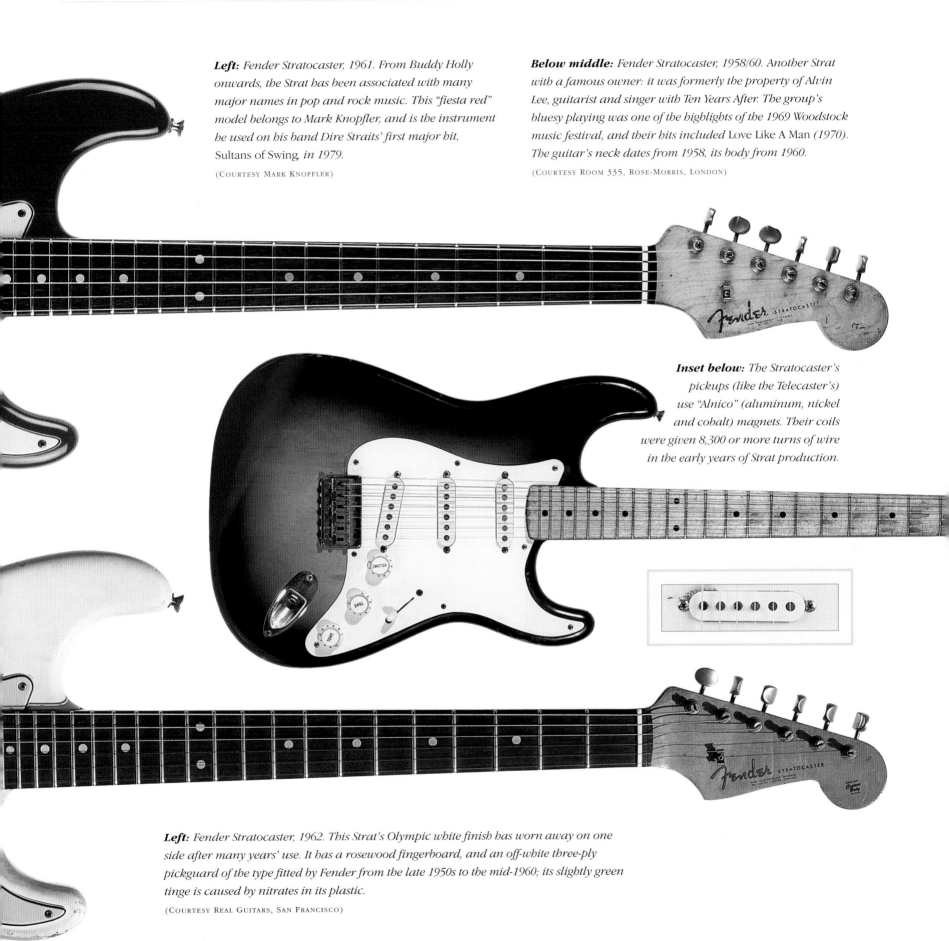

Left: *Fender Stratocaster, 1961. From Buddy Holly onwards, the Strat has been associated with many major names in pop and rock music. This "fiesta red" model belongs to Mark Knopfler, and is the instrument he used on his band Dire Straits' first major hit,* Sultans of Swing, *in 1979.*

(COURTESY MARK KNOPFLER)

Below middle: *Fender Stratocaster, 1958/60. Another Strat with a famous owner: it was formerly the property of Alvin Lee, guitarist and singer with Ten Years After. The group's bluesy playing was one of the highlights of the 1969 Woodstock music festival, and their hits included* Love Like A Man *(1970). The guitar's neck dates from 1958, its body from 1960.*

(COURTESY ROOM 335, ROSE-MORRIS, LONDON)

Inset below: *The Stratocaster's pickups (like the Telecaster's) use "Alnico" (aluminum, nickel and cobalt) magnets. Their coils were given 8,300 or more turns of wire in the early years of Strat production.*

Left: *Fender Stratocaster, 1962. This Strat's Olympic white finish has worn away on one side after many years' use. It has a rosewood fingerboard, and an off-white three-ply pickguard of the type fitted by Fender from the late 1950s to the mid-1960; its slightly green tinge is caused by nitrates in its plastic.*

(COURTESY REAL GUITARS, SAN FRANCISCO)

Les Paul and Gibson

Les Paul, born in 1916 in Waukesha, Wisconsin, was already a skilled guitarist by his teens. After achieving early fame as an acoustic player, he became attracted to the possibilities of the electric guitar during the 1930s. His musical abilities were paralleled by a strong interest in electronics; in the late 1940s, he was one of the first performers to use overdubbing on his recordings, and the subsequent hit singles he made with his wife, singer/guitarist Mary Ford, often featured double-tracking, "speeding-up," and other novel tape effects.

A few years earlier, the "Wizard of Waukesha's" curiosity about technology had led him to make a significant breakthrough in electric guitar design. In 1941, using facilities borrowed from the Epiphone company in New York, he constructed an experimental instrument that would later become famous as "The Log." After cutting up an old Epiphone archtop body, he reassembled it with a slab of solid pine in its center. This block of wood carried two home-made pickups, a bridge and a vibrato tailpiece, and the guitar was completed with an old Gibson neck and fingerboard. "The Log" proved to

Below: Gibson Les Paul, 1952. This "gold-top" model is the earliest version of the Les Paul. It has two Gibson P-90 pickups (often nicknamed "soapbars" because of their shape) and a trapeze-style bridge/tailpiece designed by Les Paul himself. (COURTESY GUITAR SHOWCASE, SAN JOSE)

Below: Gibson Les Paul Junior, 1958. The original 1952 Les Paul was joined, two years later, by "premium" and "economy" versions of the same design – the Les Paul Custom (illustrated on pages 40-41) and the "Junior" model shown here, which shares the other guitars' mahogany body and neck. Despite its single pickup and flat, uncarved body, it remains an attractive and sought-after instrument.

(COURTESY ELDERLY INSTRUMENTS:
PHOTOGRAPH BY DAVE MATCHETTE)

Above: Les Paul pictured with "The Log" – the remarkable instrument put together by the great guitarist to explore the possibilities of solid body design. It is now on display at the Country Music Hall of Fame in Nashville.

(PHOTOGRAPH COURTESY JON SIEVERT, SAN FRANCISCO)

Below: As on most Gibson electric guitars, the pickups on the Gibson Les Paul "gold top" have individual volume and tone controls, and are selected by the switch on the top left of the body. (COURTESY GUITAR SHOWCASE, SAN JOSE)

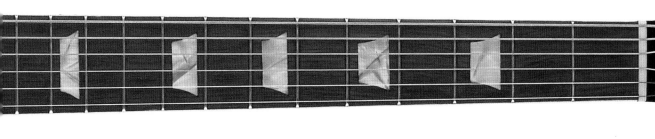

have remarkable sustain, and was also impervious to the acoustic feedback that dogged many hollow-body electrics; but despite Les Paul's efforts in the following years, he was unable to persuade anyone to manufacture it commercially.

By the early 1950s, however, the industry was more receptive to the idea of solid guitars. Foremost among the leading manufacturers eagerly developing rivals to the Fender Telecaster was Gibson, with a carved-top prototype solid that

the company's President, Ted McCarty, showed to Les Paul – then at the height of his fame as a recording artist – in about 1951. The exact role that Les played in the guitar's evolution is a matter of debate (he has always maintained that it was entirely his brainchild), although he was certainly responsible for the original tailpiece, and had some input into later modifications. He also agreed to endorse the guitar, and the Gibson Les Paul went on sale in 1952 priced $210.

The Evolution of the Gibson Les Paul

Unlike the Fender Telecaster and Stratocaster, the Gibson Les Paul underwent substantial changes to its hardware and electronics throughout the 1950s. Ironically, the first of these was the removal of the trapeze bridge/tailpiece that had been Les Paul's major contribution to the design. In 1953, it was replaced with a simpler "stud" or "stop" bridge/tailpiece attached directly to the top of the guitar. The following year, Gibson introduced its "Tune-O-Matic" bridge, invented and patented by Ted McCarty, and allowing individual string adjustment; this was incorporated onto a new model, the all-black Les Paul Custom, and subsequently fitted to the original instrument (which was later named the Les Paul Standard).

Gibson then launched another pair of Les Pauls; in contrast to their predecessors, the "Junior" (1954) and "Special" (1955) had flat, uncarved tops, but retained the simple "stop" bridge/tailpiece. The Junior had a single pickup, while the Special featured two.

The next and most important alteration was to the pickups on the two top-of-the-line models. The Les Paul's P-90s, like all previous guitar pickups, had single coils, which can be affected by interference from nearby electrical equipment. In the 1930s, when the first electric guitars appeared, electricity itself was a rarer commodity, and there were fewer problems with this kind of noise. But by the 1950s, far more

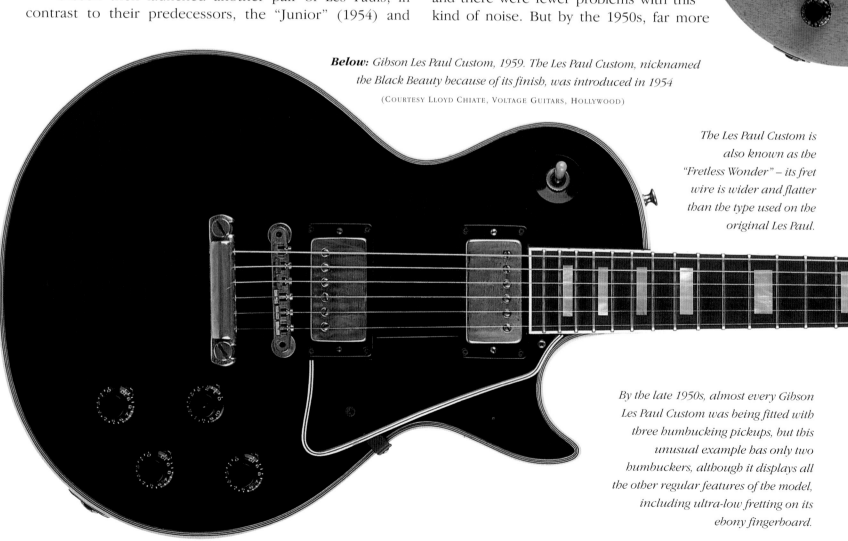

Below: Gibson Les Paul Custom, 1959. The Les Paul Custom, nicknamed the Black Beauty because of its finish, was introduced in 1954

(Courtesy Lloyd Chiate, Voltage Guitars, Hollywood)

The Les Paul Custom is also known as the "Fretless Wonder" – its fret wire is wider and flatter than the type used on the original Les Paul.

By the late 1950s, almost every Gibson Les Paul Custom was being fitted with three humbucking pickups, but this unusual example has only two humbuckers, although it displays all the other regular features of the model, including ultra-low fretting on its ebony fingerboard.

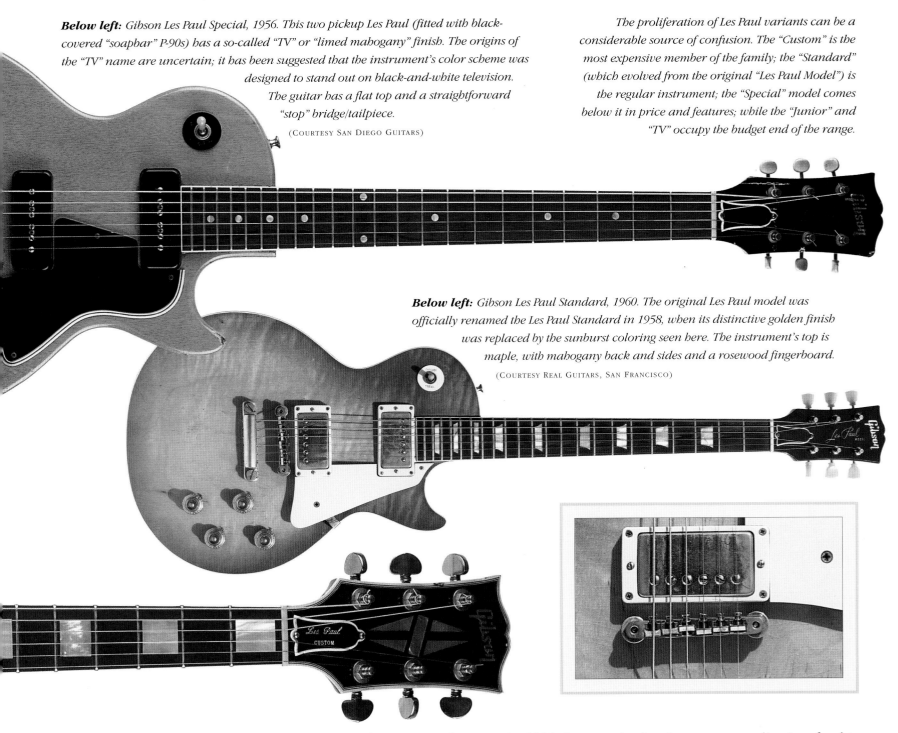

Below left: *Gibson Les Paul Special, 1956. This two pickup Les Paul (fitted with black-covered "soapbar" P-90s) has a so-called "TV" or "limed mahogany" finish. The origins of the "TV" name are uncertain; it has been suggested that the instrument's color scheme was designed to stand out on black-and-white television. The guitar has a flat top and a straightforward "stop" bridge/tailpiece.*
(COURTESY SAN DIEGO GUITARS)

The proliferation of Les Paul variants can be a considerable source of confusion. The "Custom" is the most expensive member of the family; the "Standard" (which evolved from the original "Les Paul Model") is the regular instrument; the "Special" model comes below it in price and features; while the "Junior" and "TV" occupy the budget end of the range.

Below left: *Gibson Les Paul Standard, 1960. The original Les Paul model was officially renamed the Les Paul Standard in 1958, when its distinctive golden finish was replaced by the sunburst coloring seen here. The instrument's top is maple, with mahogany back and sides and a rosewood fingerboard.*
(COURTESY REAL GUITARS, SAN FRANCISCO)

mains-driven appliances were in use, and buzzing and humming were often clearly audible – thanks in part to the increasingly powerful, higher-fidelity amplifiers and speakers now available to players. In 1954, Gibson engineer Seth Lover (1910–1997) began developing a guitar pickup containing two adjacent coils, wired out-of-phase with each other. This design canceled out ("bucked") stray electrical fields, while producing a richer tone and more powerful output from the strings.

In 1955, Lover submitted a patent application for his "humbucking" twin-coil pickup (it was granted four years later), and from 1957 onwards, humbuckers were fitted to Standard and Custom Les Pauls. While some players still favor the single-coil P-90s, it is Seth Lover's humbuckers that are responsible for the distinctive "Les Paul sound," familiar from countless rock and blues records. Replicas of both transducers are currently made by several specialist pickup manufacturers.

From Les Paul to SG

In the late 1950s, Gibson decided to make radical alterations to its Les Paul guitars. The changes started with the Junior and TV models, which were relaunched with double cutaways in 1958; the Special followed suit a year later. These modified instruments retained the 1¾-inch (4.4cm) thickness of the original design, and also continued to carry Les Paul's endorsement – at least for a while. The musician's contract with Gibson was drawing to a close; over the next few years, his name gradually disappeared from the company's headstocks and catalogs, and the "Les Paul" range was eventually given a new classification: "SG" (for "solid guitar").

The thick-bodied double cutaway design (illustrated opposite, far right) proved to be only an intermediate stage. In 1960, the Les Paul Standard was the first guitar to adopt what became known as the "classic" SG shape, with its much thinner profile and sharp-horned cutaways. The following year, this slimline style was introduced on the Custom, Special, Junior, and TV models, and the old, single cutaway Les Paul went into (temporary) retirement. However, the Standard, Junior, and Custom were not officially given the "SG" name until 1963.

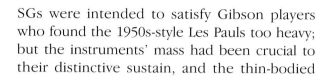

SGs were intended to satisfy Gibson players who found the 1950s-style Les Pauls too heavy; but the instruments' mass had been crucial to their distinctive sustain, and the thin-bodied SGs had a very different sound. Another significant change was the inclusion of a vibrato unit on some SG models. The earliest type (seen on the 1961 Les Paul/SG Standard opposite) had a hinged arm that was pulled from side to side; this was replaced by a Vibrola unit with an up-and-down action. SG pickup configurations corresponded to those on the Les Pauls; humbuckers were used on the Standard and Custom SGs, and single-coil P-90s on the Specials and Juniors. The SG was Gibson's first attempt at a slim, streamlined solid body design, and it has retained its popularity for 40 years. Leading players who have used it include Angus Young of AC/DC, Tony Iommi of Black Sabbath, and the late Frank Zappa.

Below and left: *Gibson Les Paul/SG Standard, 1961. An early example of the first SG model, which still carries Les Paul's name on the headstock* **(inset, above)**. *It has a mahogany body, a rosewood fingerboard, and two humbucking pickups, as well as a "Tune-O-Matic" bridge and the Gibson vibrato unit described above.*

(COURTESY LLOYD CHIATE, VOLTAGE GUITARS, HOLLYWOOD)

Left: *Gibson SG Standard, 1964. By the time this instrument was made, Les Paul and Gibson had ended their endorsement agreement, and his name had disappeared from the SG range. The vibrato unit on the guitar is the newer up-and down model, but the pickups and overall construction remain unchanged.*

(COURTESY REAL GUITARS, SAN FRANCISCO)

Far right: *Gibson SG Special, 1961. The first stage in Gibson's redesign of the Les Paul line was the introduction of this "intermediate" body shape, featuring a double cutaway but retaining the same thickness as the original Les Paul models. The Special was available in this form for about two years from 1959; in 1961 it was given the thinner, contoured SG body with its sharp-horned cutaways.*

(COURTESY MARK KNOPFLER)

The SG Special, Melody Maker and SG Junior

Sales of the old Les Paul range had been declining in the late 1950s, but Gibson's promotional literature was upbeat about the prospects for its replacement – the "ultra-thin, hand contoured double cutaway" SG design. One advertisement described the new, distinctive shape as "an exciting new approach to the solid body guitar" and quipped that it was "a solid success with players."

In fact, SGs were fairly modest sellers, due in part to the overall shift in public tastes towards folk-style music in the first years of the decade. This was not a matter of great concern to Gibson; as a highly acclaimed manufacturer of both acoustic guitars and of

electric instruments, its diversity – and sheer size – seemed to be a guarantee of its continuing success. By 1966, the company was the largest guitar maker in the world, occupying 250,000 square feet (23,225m²)of manufacturing space; and its output had expanded to include not only its own instruments, but also the less-expensive Epiphone and Kalamazoo lines. (See pages 54-55 for the history of Epiphone's assimilation by Gibson/CMI).

Gibson understood the importance of keeping its more basic models within the reach of beginners and younger players. In 1959, it launched the Melody Maker solid-body guitar, priced at only $99.50 for a single pickup version in full or ¾ sizes (a twin pickup instrument was also available). In its original form, the Melody Maker bore a close resemblance to

Below left: Gibson SG Junior, 1967. This SG Junior has a single P-90 pickup, surrounded by a black plastic pickguard – a new design brought in during 1966. (COURTESY ROD & HANK'S, MEMPHIS)

The SG Junior's bridge is a non-adjustable unit with factory-set string compensation, rather than the "Tune-O-Matic" type found on the SG Custom and Standard.

Below left: Gibson Melody Maker, 1964. One of the most distinctive features of the Melody Maker is its narrow headstock. This does not appear on the Les Paul Junior from which it took so many other characteristics, but can be found on the Epiphone Olympic (see pages 54-55), another Gibson-made solid introduced in 1960.

The Melody Maker's single pickup was specially designed for the model, but later appeared on a number of cut-price "Kalamazoo" guitars manufactured by Gibson in the late 1960s. (COURTESY GUITAR SHOWCASE, SAN JOSE)

the Les Paul Junior (see pages 38-39), but the example shown here dates from 1964 – two years after the introduction of a double cutaway. In 1967, the Melody Maker underwent some more substantial changes, acquiring an "SG" shape and also appearing in three-pickup and twelve-string configurations.

The third guitar shown here is an SG Junior – like the Melody Maker, a direct descendant of the Les Paul Junior. It acquired its SG-style body in 1961, but its electronics were essentially unchanged from its Les Paul days, with a single P-90 pickup fitted close to the bridge for a harder, punchier tone. Its

Above left: Gibson SG Special, 1965.
Like all SGs, the Special has an unbound mahogany body and neck. Its pickups are P-90 single-coils (not the humbuckers fitted to the more "upmarket" instruments in the range) and it has a Gibson Vibrola tailpiece. It is finished in cherry red – white was also available.
(COURTESY ROOM 335, ROSE-MORRIS, LONDON)

vibrato, previously an additional extra, became a standard feature in 1965, and the instrument remained in production until 1971.

The Fender Esquire, Jazzmaster and Jaguar

*I*n 1950, the single-pickup Esquire had been announced as Fender's first "electric Spanish" guitar (see pages 30-31); but after the company decided to launch the dual-pickup Broadcaster/Telecaster instead, the Esquire's debut was delayed until the following year. One curious result of the company's indecision over the specifications for the Esquire and Broadcaster is the presence of a routed-out space for the "missing" neck pickup on production Esquires. This cavity is concealed beneath the guitar's pickguard.

In most respects, the Esquire's design and finish are identical to the Telecaster's. It has a simplified version of the Tele tone-circuitry, with a three-position switch that can provide a preset "bassy" sound, and allow the instrument's rotary tone control to be used or bypassed. The Esquire continued in production until 1970; the model illustrated here dates from 1957.

The previous year, Fender had launched two smaller-size electric guitars aimed chiefly at beginners, the Musicmaster and Duo-Sonic; but its next premier model was the Jazzmaster, which appeared in 1958. It featured new pickups, a shape designed to fit the contours of the player's body even more snugly than the Stratocaster, and a "floating" vibrato system that could be disabled with a "trem-lok" to allow easy restringing and minimize tuning problems caused by string breakages.

There were initial doubts about the Jazzmaster's look and feel. Leo Fender's friend and colleague Forrest White said that at first sight, it reminded him of "a pregnant duck," and other players were put off by its considerable weight. However, the guitar proved highly successful with 1950s and 1960s pop groups, and later with punk and New Wave artists such as Elvis Costello.

Fender's follow-up to the Jazzmaster was its 1962 Jaguar model. It had many similarities to its predecessor, but was fitted with a 22-fret neck that had a shorter scale than previous full-size Fenders, and newly designed pickups incorporating notched metal screening as protection against electrical interference. It was less popular than the Jaguar, and was discontinued in 1974 – although Fender is currently producing a "reissued' version made in the Far East.

Above: Fender Jazzmaster, 1960. The body and headstock are finished in "daphne blue," and the pickguard is imitation tortoiseshell. The Jazzmaster's pickup controls allow the player to switch easily between pre-set "lead" and "rhythm" tone-colors. On this instrument, the arm controlling the patented "floating" vibrato mechanism has been removed. (COURTESY SAN DIEGO GUITARS)

Headstock of the Fender Jaguar, 1962.

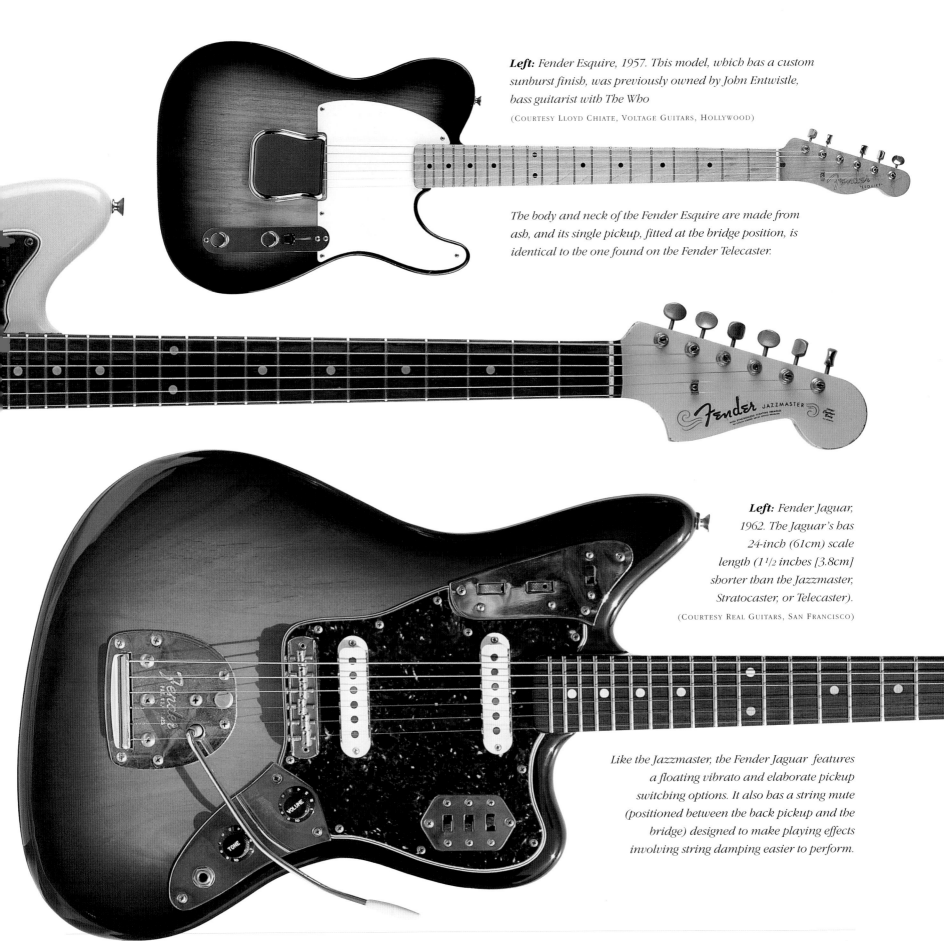

Left: Fender Esquire, 1957. This model, which has a custom sunburst finish, was previously owned by John Entwistle, bass guitarist with The Who

(COURTESY LLOYD CHIATE, VOLTAGE GUITARS, HOLLYWOOD)

The body and neck of the Fender Esquire are made from ash, and its single pickup, fitted at the bridge position, is identical to the one found on the Fender Telecaster.

Left: Fender Jaguar, 1962. The Jaguar's has 24-inch (61cm) scale length (1¹/₂ inches [3.8cm] shorter than the Jazzmaster, Stratocaster, or Telecaster).

(COURTESY REAL GUITARS, SAN FRANCISCO)

Like the Jazzmaster, the Fender Jaguar features a floating vibrato and elaborate pickup switching options. It also has a string mute (positioned between the back pickup and the bridge) designed to make playing effects involving string damping easier to perform.

The Fender Mustang and Electric XII

The Fender Mustang, introduced in 1964, was designed as a student model. It had a 24-inch (61cm) scale length, but was also available with a 22½-inch (57.15cm) scale, like Fender's other beginners' instruments, the Musicmaster and Duo-Sonic. Compared to them, however, the Mustang had a much more sophisticated range of features, including yet another new "floating" vibrato system, and the now-familiar sliding pickup switches offering a variety of tone settings.

While the other Fender student guitars are rarely used by serious performers, the Mustang has developed something of a cult following over the years. One of its more recent high-profile devotees was Kurt Cobain of Nirvana, who made it the basis for his "Jag-Stang" – the custom model

that he played from 1993 until his death a year later. In 1996, Fender put a replica of this unusual design into regular production, and it is featured on pages 110-111.

During 1965, The Byrds' *Mr. Tambourine Man* and *Turn, Turn, Turn,* featuring the distinctive tones of Jim McGuinn's twelve-string Rickenbacker, were making a major impact on the charts. The time was right for Fender to capitalize on the sound of the moment with its Electric XII model, which appeared that summer, but had been in development for some months before the CBS takeover in January. The new guitar's pickups were installed as two pairs of staggered units (an idea borrowed from the split-pickup configuration found on Fender's Precision basses from 1957 onwards). The combined tension of its extra strings made the provision of a vibrato unit impracticable; but Leo Fender's elaborate bridge design ensured that intonation could be precisely adjusted. The

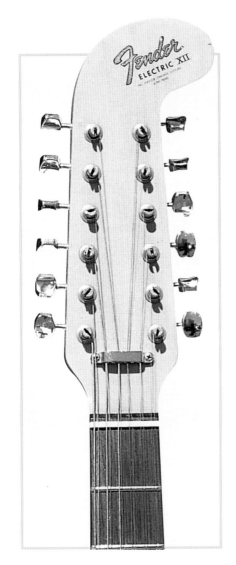

Left: Fender Electric XII, 1966. The Electric XII was one of the last designs developed during the "pre-CBS" days at Fender. Its pickups are switched by the black knob on the top right of the pickguard; they can be selected individually, combined, or fed through a pre-set tone-circuit. This example has a sunburst finish; blond and custom Fender colors were also available

Right: The Electric XII's distinctive headstock inspired its affectionate nickname – "the hockey stick." A more conventional headstock shape has been used for Fender/Squier's current Venus XII model.
(COURTESY REAL GUITARS, SAN FRANCISCO)

Electric XII was not a great success, and was withdrawn in 1969. More recently, Fender has introduced another solid-body twelve-string, the Venus XII (also available in a cheaper Squier version endorsed by Crispian Mills of Kula Shaker).

Over a 15-year period, Leo Fender and his team had created an astonishing range of superbly designed guitars. The background to Leo's departure from the company he founded, and the changes brought about by its new owners' more rigid managerial approach, are outlined in Chapter Four.

Above left: Fender Mustang, 1965. This guitar, finished in Olympic white, has a 24-inch (61cm) scale. Unlike the other Fenders designed for beginners, it has a vibrato unit – a new design patented by Leo Fender in 1966, with a floating bridge that moves backwards and forwards when the unit is activated. The two single-coil pickups are angled for optimum bass and treble response.
(COURTESY LLOYD CHIATE, VOLTAGE GUITARS, HOLLYWOOD)

Sears and Danelectro

eo Fender's designs stimulated demand for the electric guitar at all levels. His "flagship" models, including the Telecaster and Stratocaster, attracted professionals and serious players, while his student instruments were priced within reach of reasonably well-heeled beginners – or their parents! But by the mid-1950s, even cheaper electric guitars and amplifiers were readily available, thanks to the buying power and marketing muscle of America's premier sales catalog company: Sears, Roebuck, and Company.

Sears had been selling musical instruments since well before World War I, and in 1954 it launched its first electric Spanish solid-bodied guitars. These carried the Sears "Silvertone" label, but were actually made by a variety of outside contractors, including Harmony, Kay, and Nathan Daniel, an innovative New Jersey-based designer. Daniel (1912–1994) had been Sears' exclusive amp manufacturer since 1948, and his company, Danelectro, also supplied equipment to a number of other leading wholesalers.

The earliest Silvertone solids had poplar bodies; Daniel produced them in single and double pickup versions, and soon afterwards began selling similar models under his own Danelectro trademark. In 1956, he changed the design and construction of his guitars. The second generation of Silvertone/Danelectros still had poplar or pine sides, necks, and bridge blocks, but for their tops and backs, Daniel started using Masonite – a cheap hardboard material containing wood chips and fiber, mixed with resin. The guitars' finish and hardware were also highly unconventional; their sides were coated with Naugahide (a durable plastic often used on chair-seats), and the metal pickup covers were made from surplus chrome-plated lipstick tubes.

Nathan Daniel fashioned these odd ingredients into strikingly effective designs. One of his Silvertone guitar outfits featured an amp and speaker built into the instrument's case, while his Danelectro and later Coral ranges offered innovative body shapes, the first-ever six-string bass, and even a hybrid sitar guitar. Sadly, his company went out of business in 1969; but there is still considerable demand for his instruments, and since the mid-1980s, Jerry Jones Guitars of Nashville, Tennessee, has been making high-quality reproductions of the Danelectro line. Its work is featured on pages 122-123.

Below left: *Danelectro "Convertible" – early 1960s. As its name suggests, this ingenious guitar is designed to be equally suitable for electric and acoustic playing, with a single pickup fitted across its soundhole. It has the distinctive double-cutaway "Shorthorn" body shape first used by Nathan Daniel for his Danelectros and Silvertones in the late 1950s.*

(COURTESY GUITAR SHOWCASE, SAN JOSE)

Opposite page and inset, right: *Danelectro U-2, 1957 (serial number 5047). In 1956, Nathan Daniel launched his U-1 and U-2 models – the former has a single pickup, the latter has two. They were the first of his guitars to be built using Masonite, and another unusual feature is the use, on the U-2, of concentric volume/tone controls, with the two knobs for each pickup stacked on top of each other.*

(FROM THE COLLECTION OF DOUG TULLOCH, CITY GUITAR, NEW BEDFORD, MA: PHOTOGRAPH BY DOUG TULLOCH)

Left: *Danelectro Pro 1 – c.1965. The Pro 1 has an unusual "bow-tie" outline not found on any other Danelectros, and is fitted with a single "lipstick-tube" pickup. The model was introduced in 1963, and stayed in production for the remaining six years of the company's life.*

(COURTESY REAL GUITARS, SAN FRANCISCO)

Solid Guitars by Gretsch and Rickenbacker

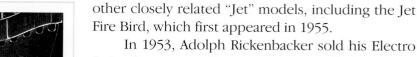

The Fred Gretsch company of Brooklyn, New York, was a long established and highly respected manufacturer and distributor, famous for its drums and fretted instruments. Gretsch had been making electric archtop guitars since the 1940s, but was initially skeptical to the point of derision about solid-bodies. When Gibson introduced the Les Paul in 1952, Fred Gretsch Jnr. phoned Gibson President Ted McCarty to express his horror at the move, commenting that "now anyone with a band saw can make a guitar."

Nevertheless, only two years later Gretsch launched its own electric solid-bodied guitar, the Duo-Jet. It had some similarities to the Les Paul, but used a different body construction (see caption) and, like other Gretsch electrics of the period, was fitted with pickups made by DeArmond, which had made its early reputation with removable "floating" pickup assemblies for acoustic archtops. The Duo-Jet went through a number of subsequent design changes, eventually acquiring a double cutaway body and a pair of Gretsch's own twin-coil "Filter-'Tron" pickups. The company also produced several other closely related "Jet" models, including the Jet Fire Bird, which first appeared in 1955.

In 1953, Adolph Rickenbacker sold his Electro String Instrument Company to F.C. Hall (founder of Radio-Tel, the original distributor of Leo Fender's guitars), and soon afterwards, work began on a new line of Rickenbacker solid-bodies, named the "Combo" range. The first Combo guitar emerged a year later, and the instrument opposite, the distinctively tulip-shaped Combo 450, made its debut in 1957. The 450, and its single-pickup version, the 400, quickly found favor with distinguished jazz musician Toots Thielemans (b.1922), who used them while working with the George Shearing Quintet. The instruments also attracted the attention of the young John Lennon; according to John C. Hall, who has succeeded his father as Chairman and CEO of Rickenbacker, it was the sound of Thielemans playing a "Tulip" that prompted Lennon to visit a Hamburg music store and order a Rickenbacker of his own – although the guitar he eventually acquired was not the 450 but the "thin hollow body" Model 325 he made famous with The Beatles.

Above right: Gretsch Jet Fire Bird, 1965. This 1960s version of the Jet Fire Bird has a double cutaway and two Gretsch "Filter-'Tron" pickups; it retains the body cavity of the original Duo-Jet. **Inset, right:** The "thumbprint" position markers on the neck are a characteristic Gretsch feature, also found on many of their semi-acoustic models (see pages 72-75).

(COURTESY ERIC SCHOENBERG)

Left: Rickenbacker Combo 450, 1957. The Combo 450 appeared a few months after the 400, a single-pickup model with the same body design. The 400 and 450 were the first Rickenbackers to use neck-through-body construction, in which a single piece of wood is used for the entire center section of the instrument from headstock to tail. This 450 is finished in jet black; brown and green were also available.

(COURTESY RICKENBACKER INTERNATIONAL CORPORATION)

Right: *Gretsch Duo-Jet, 1956. Unlike the Gibson Les Paul, which has a similar body shape, the Duo-Jet is not completely solid, but has a substantial cavity inside its mahogany body. The model is associated with several famous players, notably George Harrison, who frequently used one with the Beatles.*
(COURTESY GUITAR SHOWCASE, SAN JOSE)

Solid Guitars by Epiphone

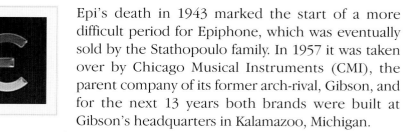

piphone, like Gretsch, had been a major name in American instrument building for many years. The company was a family business, founded in New York by a Greek émigré, Anastasios Stathopoulo, in 1873, and originally known as the House of Stathopoulo. The Epiphone name came from Anastasios' son, Epaminondas (Epi), who took control of the firm in 1928; under his management, it had excelled in archtop guitar manufacture throughout the 1930s and early 1940s.

Epi's death in 1943 marked the start of a more difficult period for Epiphone, which was eventually sold by the Stathopoulo family. In 1957 it was taken over by Chicago Musical Instruments (CMI), the parent company of its former arch-rival, Gibson, and for the next 13 years both brands were built at Gibson's headquarters in Kalamazoo, Michigan.

As former Gibson President Ted McCarty explained in an interview for "The Gibson," published in 1996, several existing Epiphone designs continued in production under the new

***Below:** Epiphone Olympic, 1961. The Olympic was introduced in 1960 – the year after the Gibson Melody Maker with which it shares many similarities. Early versions of both models feature one single-coil pickup mounted in the bridge position, and a characteristic cutaway body with a Les Paul-like outline.*

(COURTESY ROOM 335, ROSE-MORRIS, LONDON)

regime. "We shipped the entire factory to Kalamazoo and began making Epiphones in exact accordance with the original plans for those guitars." But McCarty also had other ideas for CMI's new acquisition: "Epiphone…was a useful marketing tool as we could sell the Epiphone line to the newer dealers and keep selling Gibson guitars to loyal Gibson dealers….They were a companion line for Gibson but not an exact copy and fitted perfectly with our plans."

Effectively, McCarty's approach was to make Epiphone instruments a slightly cheaper complement to the Gibson range. He began introducing new Epiphone models soon after the takeover, and some of them had strong similarities to more upmarket Gibson designs. For example, the Epiphone Olympics illustrated opposite closely resemble Gibson's Melody Maker solid-bodies (see pages 44-45). However, other Epiphones have no direct Gibson counterpart; among these is the Crestwood also shown here, which was probably aimed at would-be Gibson SG owners whose finances could not stretch to the more expensive model.

In 1970, Gibson changed their policy over Epiphone, discontinuing U.S. manufacture of the range and transferring its production to the Far East.

Left: Epiphone Crestwood, 1962. The Crestwood was the first of the Kalamazoo-designed Epiphone solids; it was launched in 1958 and underwent a number of design changes over the following 12 years. Its two humbucking pickups are smaller and lower in output than those found on Gibson instruments.

(COURTESY LLOYD CHIATE, VOLTAGE GUITARS, HOLLYWOOD)

Left: Epiphone Olympic, 1966. By 1961, the Gibson Melody Maker had gained a double cutaway, and a year later the same feature appeared on the Epiphone Olympic, which – like its Gibson counterpart – was also available in one- or two-pickup versions, and with a vibrato arm.

(COURTESY ROD & HANK'S, MEMPHIS)

CHAPTER 3
THE HOLLOW-BODY AND SEMI-SOLID ELECTRIC 1946–1965

Since the introduction of the ground-breaking L-5 in 1922, Gibson had been steadily developing its archtop range; however, its earliest amplified archtops, such as the successful ES-150 (see pages 20-21) were essentially acoustic instruments with added pickups, rather than thoroughgoing electric designs. This was soon to change after World War II, when the company began to adopt a different approach to the construction of these models.

In 1946, Gibson resumed production of the ES-150 and two other hollow-body electrics, the ES-125 and ES-300. The reissued guitars were made from laminated wood, not solid timbers, and their tops were no longer carved, but pressed into shape. There were a number of reasons for this apparently retrograde step. Carving guitar tops was slow and labour-intensive, and Gibson's new owners, Chicago Musical Instruments (CMI), were keen to increase production levels. Premium-quality tonewoods were scarcer and more expensive than they had been before the war; and, significantly, some designers felt that solid wood was not necessary for a good electric sound. Gibson went on to use laminates for the majority of its post-war archtop designs.

Another departure was the inclusion of cutaways on the company's electric archtop bodies, allowing easier access to the higher reaches of their fingerboards. Gibson used two styles of cutaway: the rounded "Venetian" type found on its first-ever electric cutaway model, the ES-350P, which appeared

in 1947; and the sharper "Florentine" shape used for another new model, the ES-175, that was launched two years later.

The 175 proved to be one of the most important electric archtops ever to come out of Kalamazoo. It was modestly priced ($175), and fitted with a single pickup in the neck position (a dual pickup version appeared in 1953). The 175's deep body and warm, rich sound made it especially appealing to jazz players; Kenny Burrell was among the first major names to use it, and it has subsequently been associated with Joe Pass, Herb Ellis, Pat Metheny, and many others. Over the years, it has also attracted a number of leading rock guitarists (including Steve Howe of Yes, and Mark Knopfler of Dire Straits), and it remains in production today.

Right: Gibson ES-175, 1958. Its 16-inch (40.6cm) top is made from laminated spruce; the back and sides are laminated maple, and the neck is mahogany. This model has a humbucking pickup – earlier ES-175s had been fitted with P-90 single-coil units. The one-pickup version of the 175 was eventually discontinued in 1972.

(COURTESY MARK KNOPFLER)

Below left: Gibson ES-175D, 1961. The "D" suffix denotes a double-pickup model. In 1956, three years after its introduction, the 175D gained a new T-shaped tailpiece **(opposite page, inset)** with zigzag metal tubing on either side.

(COURTESY GUITAR SHOWCASE, SAN JOSE)

Right: *Gibson ES-175D, 1965. Unlike the 1961 guitar, this sunburst-finish model is fitted with an original-style trapeze tailpiece. The ES-175 has now become the longest surviving and best-selling archtop in the Gibson catalog.*

(COURTESY MARK KNOPFLER)

The Gibson ES-5 and L-5CES

The ES-175 was not the only new Gibson archtop unveiled in 1949. The other major design launched by the company that year was its ES-5, a "supreme electronic" version of the acoustic L-5 model, fitted with no fewer than three P-90 pickups.

The ES-5's introduction was a clear indication that Gibson now saw its amplified archtops as true electric guitars, not acoustics with pickups. Mounting a trio of bulky P-90s onto its laminated top inevitably had an detrimental effect on its "unplugged" tone, but provided a remarkable range of electric sounds. Gibson's publicity proclaimed the ES-5 an "instrument of a thousand voices;" its neck pickup gave a warm, "rhythm guitar" timbre, while the other two trans-ducers were positioned to emphasize the middle and treble frequencies. Each pickup had a separate volume knob, allowing the player to mix the sounds together, and there was an overall tone control mounted on the instrument's upper right-hand bout.

Surprisingly, the original ES-5 had no selector switching; and many players must have found its rotary volume knobs awkward to manage when quick changes of sound were

required. Gibson's solution was to introduce a modified version of the instrument, named the "Switchmaster," in 1955. This offered separate volume and tone controls for each pickup, and a four-way lever selecting individual pickups or all three simultaneously.

For lovers of the L-5 who wanted less elaborate electronics, Gibson produced the

Right: Gibson ES-5, 1951. The ES-5's 17-inch (43.2cm)-wide top, as well as its sides and back, are made from laminated maple. Like most Gibson archtops of the period, it was available in a blonde "natural" finish (as shown here) or in sunburst. (COURTESY MARK KNOPFLER)

L-5CES (the C stands for "cutaway") in 1951. This guitar, one of the two "flagships" of the Electric Spanish range (together with the Super 400CES – see pages 60-61) was among the few post-war Gibson electric hollowbodies to retain a carved solid spruce top. When the instrument first appeared, it was fitted with two P-90 pickups. These were later replaced by Alnico V single-coils, and, in 1958, by Gibson's newly developed humbuckers (see pages 40-41); these can be seen on the instrument below, which dates from 1961.

The L-5CES has had many devotees among famous jazzmen, among them Wes Montgomery, Oscar Moore (guitarist with the Nat King Cole Trio), and Mundell Lowe.

Left: Gibson ES-5 Switchmaster, 1957. This version of the ES-5 was designed to make pickup selection and control easier for players.

(COURTESY MARK KNOPFLER)

Apart from the four-way switch, fitted to the Gibson ES-5 Switchmaster in place of the master tone control, the only significant difference between the Switchmaster and the original ES-5 is the newer instrument's more elaborate tailpiece.

Left: Gibson L-5CES, 1961. Like the later versions of its acoustic predecessor, this luxury electric hollowbody has a 17-inch (43.2cm) carved spruce top, with maple back and sides.

The cherry red color of the model shown here was introduced in 1959, and was only available to customers for two years.

(COURTESY LLOYD CHIATE, VOLTAGE GUITARS, HOLLYWOOD)

The Gibson Super 400CES and ES-295

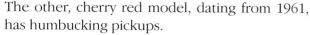

he Super 400 acoustic had been a landmark model for Gibson when it first appeared in 1934. At $400, it was the most expensive guitar the company had ever produced, and it was given an appropriately opulent finish, including gold-plated tuning machines and fine pearl inlays. It was also the largest archtop of its time, with a lower body width of 18 inches (45.7cm) subsequently exceeded only by the Epiphone Emperor (1936) and Elmer Stromberg's 19-inch (48.3cm) Master 400 (1937). Such increased body sizes were a by-product of the constant search for extra acoustic volume and power, and the coming of amplification had, to some extent, rendered them unnecessary. However, this had little effect on the popularity of the Super 400, and in 1951, Gibson introduced a new two-pickup electric version of its classic design. It cost $470, and became once again the highest-priced model in the catalog.

The Super 400CES was launched simultaneously with the L-5CES, and shared its carved, solid-top construction. The natural finish example shown opposite was one of the first Super 400s to be fitted with Gibson's Alnico V pickups, which were beginning to supersede the original P-90 units in 1953.

The other, cherry red model, dating from 1961, has humbucking pickups.

The idea of producing electric equivalents of its finest archtop acoustics was a logical and highly lucrative move on Gibson's part. But in 1952, it made a more surprising addition to its electric hollow-body range. This was the ES-295, whose all-gold finish, white pickup covers and distinctive bridge/tailpiece strongly resembled the company's new Les Paul solid, launched the same year. The 295's appearance was also reminiscent of the ES-175, with the same sharp-edged "Florentine" cutaway and "double-parallelogram" fingerboard inlays. The model remained in production for only six years; Gibson felt that its gold-colored body and neck were contributing to its unpopularity with players, and, as A.R. Duchossoir explains in his book *Gibson Electrics – The Classic Years,* the introduction of red and grey ES-295s was briefly considered. However, the idea was quickly abandoned, and no more ES-295s were built after 1958.

*Opposite page, top left: Gibson ES-295, c.1952. A striking but relatively short-lived electric archtop. Its combination bridge/tailpiece was "borrowed" from the original "gold-top" solid Les Paul Model, while its body shape resembles the ES-175, and the gold-inlaid engraving on its white pickguard **(above, inset)** is copied from a Gibson lap steel instrument.*

(COURTESY GUITAR SHOWCASE, SAN JOSE)

Left: Gibson Super 400CES, 1961. This later Super 400 has humbucking pickups and a "Florentine" cutaway, but retains the original model's elaborate inlays, engraved tailpiece, and "marbled" pickguard.

(COURTESY LLOYD CHIATE, VOLTAGE GUITARS, HOLLYWOOD)

Opposite page, far right: Gibson Super 400CES, 1953. In the words of Gibson's own publicity, the Super 400CES offered "the tonal quality of an acoustic guitar with the advantages of an electric instrument." The Alnico V pickups seen on this model were invented by Gibson's Seth Lover; they had larger magnets and a higher electrical output than the P-90s fitted to the first Super 400s. (COURTESY MARK KNOPFLER)

Below: Headstock
of the 1953 Gibson
Super 400CES.

The First Gibson "Thinlines"

"What would you like in a guitar that we don't already have?" This intriguing question was posed by a Gibson staffer to Hank Garland and Billy Byrd, two of Nashville's leading 1950s session musicians, at a disc jockey convention held in Music City in 1955. During a later interview with *Guitar Player* magazine, Garland recalled that he and Byrd "sat down [with the Gibson executive] and said we'd like an instrument like the L-5, but with a thin body and a bunch of other stuff. He wrote it all down on a piece of paper, and after he went back to…the Gibson factory, they made the guitar and sent us one."

Garland and Byrd were influential and highly respected in country music and beyond it. Byrd was famous for his work with singer Ernest Tubb, Garland had been closely associated with another star vocalist, Eddy Arnold ("The Tennessee Plowboy"), and the two men also had a strong involvement in jazz. The model they inspired, named the Byrdland in their honor, was announced only a few months after their first discussions with Gibson; it went on sale in 1956, and represented an important new direction for the company's archtop line.

While it retained the L-5's carved spruce top and outline, its reduced depth – 2¼ inches (5.7cm) as opposed to the L-5 and Super 400's 3⅜ inches (8.6cm) – gave it a much less bulky feel, particularly for guitarists who preferred to play standing up. It also had a shorter scale length, designed, as Gibson put it, "for the fast action needed in modern playing." The Byrdland was an immediate success, and has proved popular with a wide range of performers, from jazzman Barry Galbraith (with whom Hank Garland subsequently worked and studied in New York) to hard rocker Ted Nugent.

Gibson's commitment to "thinline" bodies was confirmed with the launch of two other 1955 models, the ES-350T and the less-expensive ES-225T. The following year, Gibson issued a thinline version of an already smaller-than-average guitar, the ES-140. This ¾-size instrument had first appeared in 1950; designed, according to Gibson's publicity, "principally for youngsters but ideal for any…guitarist with small fingers," it remained in production until 1968.

Right: Gibson ES-350T, c.1958. A thinline version of Gibson's 1947 ES-350 archtop. It is more than an inch (2.5cm) shallower than the original, and is fitted with two humbucking pickups, a "Tune-O-Matic" bridge and a redesigned tailpiece.
(Courtesy Mark Knopfler)

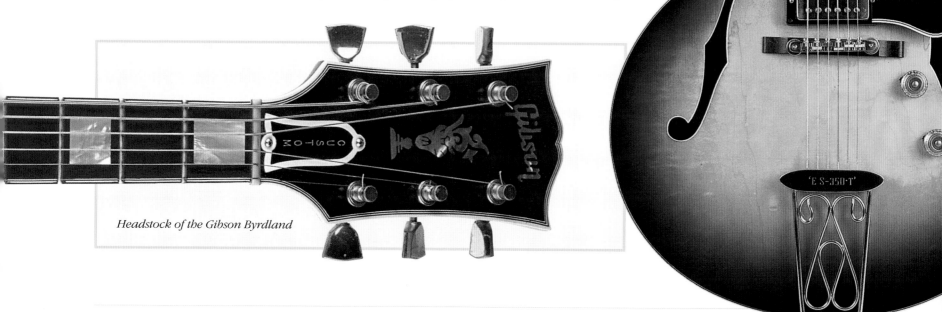

Headstock of the Gibson Byrdland

Above: *Gibson Byrdland, 1964. This Byrdland is a 17-inch (43.2cm) archtop with a spruce top, maple sides, and a laminated maple back and neck; the fingerboard is ebony. The original 1956 model had Alnico V pickups and a rounded "Venetian" cutaway. Two years later, the Alnicos were replaced by humbuckers, while the cutaway shape was changed to the sharper Florentine style in 1960.*
(COURTESY LLOYD CHIATE, VOLTAGE GUITARS, HOLLYWOOD)

Left: *Gibson ES-140T (³/₄ size), c.1960. The first publicity shots for the 140 showed it against the outline of an ES-175, and the instrument is effectively a scaled-down, single-pickup replica of that classic design.*
(COURTESY AMANDA'S TEXAS UNDERGROUND, NASHVILLE)

The Gibson ES-335

The first thinline archtop models paved the way for an even more radical Gibson design – the ES-335 "semi-solid," introduced in 1958. Its inspiration may have been Les Paul's experimental "Log" guitar of 1941, which had a central wood block supporting its pickups, bridge, and strings (see pages 38-39). The "Log" offered remarkable sustain and practically no risk of acoustic feedback, but had been rejected by Gibson after Paul showed the company the prototype.

The ES-335 featured a refined and improved version of the same basic approach. Outwardly, it looked like a standard thinline archtop, although its double cutaway was an unfamiliar sight on a Gibson instrument. Internally, there were a number of other surprises. The two outer sections of the 335's body were hollow, but at its center was a strip of maple, with glued-in pieces of spruce above and below it. These were cut to the shape of the instrument's top and back, sealing off its hollow sides. Two humbucking pickups, a "Tune-O-Matic" bridge, and a "stud" or "stop" tailpiece were all mounted on this central section. Their positioning contributed to the guitar's highly distinctive sound, which was modified and enriched by the arched top and the side cavities, but had almost as much sustain and freedom from feedback as a solid-bodied instrument's.

The 335 was an important landmark in electric instrument technology. Its innovative body design was complemented by a slim, comfortable neck with unrivaled access to the top of the scale; all 22 frets could be reached with ease, and the action was as fast and light as a Les Paul's. At a basic price of $267.50 for a sunburst model (natural finish 335s were $15 dearer) it quickly became a best seller, and was subsequently used by a host of leading names in jazz, blues, and rock. Although it has been in continuous production since 1958, many musicians and collectors believe that the earliest 335s are superior to later models. The three examples shown here are so-called "dot" 335s, made before 1962, when Gibson replaced the original fingerboard dot position markers with block inlays.

1959 Gibson ES-335TD headstock.

Below left: *Gibson ES-335TD, 1959. A sunburst ES-335 from the same early period as the other two instruments. Later, a cherry red finish was available on the model as an optional extra.* (COURTESY REAL GUITARS, SAN FRANCISCO)

Below: *Gibson ES-335TD, 1958. This beautiful early 335 is unusual in having no neck binding – standard models are edged with single-ply plastic around their fingerboards. The guitar's other features – a*

16-inch (40.6cm) laminated maple body, twin humbuckers with individual volume and tone controls, and a three-way pickup selector switch – are as normal. (COURTESY MARK KNOPFLER)

Left: *Gibson ES-335TD, 1959. Both this 335 and its companion above are nominally "natural finish" guitars. However, their differing shades demonstrate the varying degrees of "blondeness" found from model to model.* (COURTESY MARK KNOPFLER)

"Artist" Guitars

The approach to Billy Byrd and Hank Garland that led to the creation of Gibson's "Byrdland" archtop was not an isolated occurrence. Instrument makers retained close links with their distinguished customers, and fully appreciated the value of an endorsement, or a "signature" model, in boosting sales and generating publicity. Gibson's position as the inventors and premier manufacturers of archtop guitars gave it a special advantage in this area, and during the early 1960s, its President, Ted McCarty, capitalized on it by commissioning a series of "Artist" hollowbodies bearing the names of leading performers.

One of the first of these was the Gibson "Johnny Smith," launched in 1961. Smith (b.1922), a self-taught guitarist who also excelled as a trumpeter and arranger, had helped to define the "cool jazz" movement with his 1952 album *Moonlight in Vermont,* and was greatly admired as a player and bandleader. A meticulous man, he gave the company precise instructions about the design of his instrument, insisting that its acoustic tone should not be compromised by fitting any pickups or controls directly onto the top. Instead, the Johnny Smith had a

"floating" humbucker attached to the end of the guitar's neck, and a volume control built into its pickguard. The single pickup Johnny Smith was joined two years later by a double pickup version; both instruments remained in the Gibson catalog until the 1980s.

Following the success of the Smith guitar and the Gibson "Barney Kessel" archtop that appeared at the same time, McCarty introduced a third "Artist" model in 1962. Developed in collaboration with virtuoso bebop player Tal Farlow (1921–1998), this was a 17-inch (43.2cm), two-pickup instrument with a Venetian cutaway inlaid to resemble a scroll; like the Johnny Smith and Barney Kessel, it featured a "personalized" tailpiece displaying the endorsee's name.

Other archtop makers were also active in producing "signature" guitars. Gretsch's association with distinguished Nashville-based player and producer Chet Atkins (b.1924) is detailed on pages 74-75, while one of rock and roll's earliest heroes, Duane Eddy (b.1938) had an elegant archtop carrying his name designed and made by the New York-based Guild company. A 1962 example of this model is shown opposite.

Above and left: *Gibson Johnny Smith, 1963. The Johnny Smith was designed as a true acoustic/electric, and its humbucking pickup and volume control have no contact with its solid spruce top. The instrument's back, sides and neck are made from maple. Gibson continued to produce the guitar until the end of the 1980s.*

(COURTESY PAUL LEADER)

Below: *Gibson Tal Farlow, 1964. A full-depth, 17-inch (43.2cm) archtop with a laminated maple top, back and sides, and a rosewood fingerboard. Despite its elegant looks and Tal Farlow's active association with it, the instrument was not very successful, and was withdrawn in the late 1960s.*
(COURTESY LLOYD CHIATE, VOLTAGE GUITARS, HOLLYWOOD)

Above: *Headstock of the 1963 Johnny Smith*

Left: *Guild Duane Eddy, 1962. Eddy's twangy, echo-laden sound was produced using a variety of guitars; despite his endorsement of this Guild model, he is probably most closely associated with Gretsch instruments. The heavy-duty Bigsby vibrato unit fitted to the tailpiece was a favorite with many 1950s and 1960s players.*
(COURTESY LLOYD CHIATE, VOLTAGE GUITARS, HOLLYWOOD)

Epiphone Electric Archtops
1951–1963

Most of Epiphone's classic archtop designs were introduced before World War II, and those that remained in production during the post-war period underwent a number of significant changes to their specifications. The first instrument shown here is a very unusual example of this; it is a 1951 version of a lower-price model, the Byron, which made its initial appearance in about 1939. Originally, the Byron was a non-cutaway acoustic; cutaways only began to be used by Epiphone in the late 1940s, and the company normally favored the rounded, Venetian style, as seen on the Emperor guitar also illustrated opposite. However, this 1951 Byron has a sharper Florentine cutaway, as well as a pickup that appears to have been factory-fitted, although the guitar is not listed as an electric model in any of the standard vintage guitar guides. It retains the relatively small body size, "center-dip" headstock, and single trapeze tailpiece found on its pre-war namesake; during this period, Epiphone only fitted its double-trapeze "Frequensator" tailpiece to higher-end guitars.

The Emperor was the flagship of Epiphone's archtop range, launched in 1936 in direct competition to Gibson's Super 400. In 1952, Epiphone produced an electric cutaway version of the instrument fitted with three pickups, hoping to provide an attractive alternative to would-be Gibson ES-5 purchasers. When Gibson took over Epiphone in 1957, it retained the Emperor's pickup configuration, but made it a thinline model, and later replaced its "New York-style" pickups with its own "mini-humbucker" units. The Emperor was discontinued in 1970.

As well as preserving and adapting designs from the company's earlier history, Gibson introduced a number of entirely new Epiphones during the 1960s. One of the oddest of these was the Professional, which made its debut in 1962. Its double-cutaway body is reminiscent of the Gibson 335, but there is only one pickup, controlled by two standard knobs on the

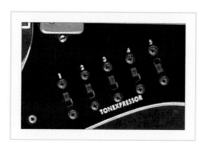

bottom right of the pickguard. The knobs and miniature switches on the opposite side allow the player to adjust volume, tone, and various effects on a separate amplifier unit. This concept was not especially successful, and in 1967 the Professional was dropped from the Epiphone catalog.

Below: Epiphone Byron, 1951. The Byron, with its relatively small 15 3/8-inch (39cm) width, was at the lower end of the Epiphone range; however, it is a highly attractive instrument with a solid spruce top and a mahogany body. Because of its unusual Florentine cutaway, this model would be worth more than $1,000 to a vintage guitar collector.

(COURTESY SAN DIEGO GUITARS)

Top left and detail, right: *Epiphone Emperor, 1961. In contrast to the Byron, the Emperor was the largest and most expensive Epiphone archtop, whose 18¹/₂-inch (47cm) top eclipsed even the Gibson Super 400 for size. This example is fitted with the "mini-humbucking" pickups designed by Seth Lover and used on a number of other "Gibson-Epiphones."*

(COURTESY LLOYD CHIATE, VOLTAGE GUITARS, HOLLYWOOD)

Top right and opposite page, inset: *Epiphone Professional, 1963. The Professional, in production from 1962–1967, was intended for use with its own amplifier, and the player can control the amp's tremolo, vibrato, and five "Tonexpressor" settings directly from the instrument.*

(COURTESY LLOYD CHIATE, VOLTAGE GUITARS, HOLLYWOOD)

The Rickenbacker 300 Series

*I*n 1956, Rickenbacker celebrated its first 25 years in the guitar-making business. The company already had a distinguished track record, and now its new owner, F.C. Hall, was nurturing plans for an exciting and innovative line of electric archtops. Initially known as the Capri series, and later as the 300 series, it was soon to bring Rickenbacker international recognition – and some very famous customers from the world of pop and rock.

The Capri/300 series guitars were designed by Roger Rossmeisl, a German émigré who had previously worked, like his father, at Gibson. Rossmeisl took charge of the wood shop at Rickenbacker's Los Angeles factory, where he developed a variety of single- and double-cutaway, thin- and full-bodied models in an integrated "house style" that made them instantly recognizable.

The range divides into a number of distinct types and classifications, though all Capri/300s share the characteristic sloping Rickenbacker headstock, and are made from maple with rosewood fingerboards. The earliest guitar illustrated here is a natural-finish pre-1958 Deluxe. "Deluxe" Rickenbackers, whether they are single-cutaway "full-body" instruments like this one, or thinner double cutaway designs, all have triangular fingerboard inlays and bound bodies.

After 1958, the company began to use numbers and suffixes for its various Capri/300 models, and the three-pickup single cutaway instrument also shown below, which dates from 1960, was given the designation 375F. (Numbers from 360 to 375 were assigned to Deluxe models, and the "F" stands for [thin] "full-body.") The third guitar illustrated is a Rickenbacker 330, a "standard" thin hollow-body model with dot fingerboard inlays and no binding.

The 300 series had even more impact on musicians than Rickenbacker's popular Combo range of solid-body guitars. A key factor in this popularity was the instruments' adoption by The Beatles; after John Lennon acquired his Model 325 in Hamburg (see pages 52-53), George Harrison began to use a twelve-string 360, and later, Paul McCartney would frequently be seen with a Rickenbacker 4001 bass. Leading American groups were also attracted to the 300 series, and we shall be looking in more detail at their choice of models in Chapter Four.

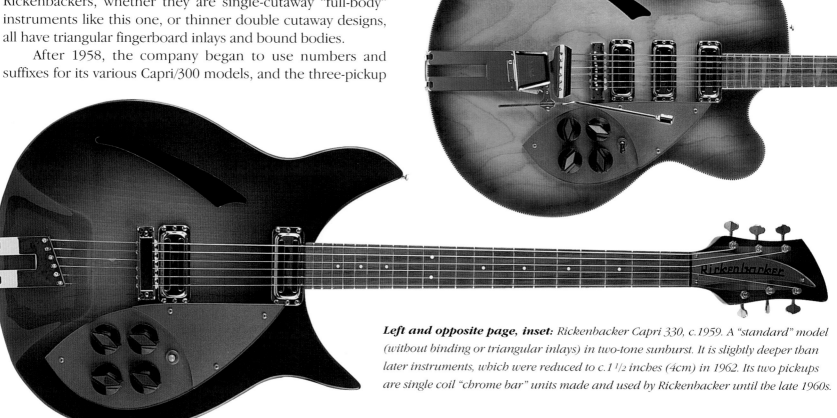

Left and opposite page, inset: Rickenbacker Capri 330, c.1959. A "standard" model (without binding or triangular inlays) in two-tone sunburst. It is slightly deeper than later instruments, which were reduced to c.1 1/2 inches (4cm) in 1962. Its two pickups are single coil "chrome bar" units made and used by Rickenbacker until the late 1960s.

Right: *Rickenbacker Capri Deluxe, pre-1958. This guitar dates from before the advent of numerical classification for Rickenbackers, but shares the specifications of an "F" (thin full-body) Deluxe series instrument.*

The Capri Deluxe has a 17-inch (43.2cm) body and is c.2 ½ inches (6.35cm) deep. The "slash" soundhole found on Rickenbacker archtops is a distinctively "European" feature, first used by the German Framus company and also made famous by American archtop luthier Jimmy D'Aquisto.

Opposite page, above left:
Rickenbacker 375F, 1960. A three-pickup thin full-body model incorporating a "vibrola" of the type originally developed by Doc Kauffman for Electro String/Rickenbacker in the 1930s (see pages 26ff.) In the 1960s, this was superseded by a more modern "Ac'cent" unit, while non-vibrato Rickenbackers had their plain "flat" tailpieces replaced with ones bearing the "R" trademark.

(ALL GUITARS ON THIS PAGE COURTESY OF
RICKENBACKER INTERNATIONAL CORPORATION)

Gretsch – from Electromatic to Double Anniversary

Gretsch's first electric archtop, the "Electromatic Spanish" guitar, appeared in 1940, but no examples or precise specifications of it are known to survive. Nine years later, the company introduced a higher-profile single pickup instrument bearing the same name; this was followed in 1951 by the Electro II – offered in 17-inch (43.2cm) cutaway and 16-inch (40.6cm) non-cutaway versions – and the 16-inch Electromatic, which was available with one or two pickups. In 1954 the Electromatic became the Streamliner, while the cutaway Electro II was renamed the Country Club.

These guitars were relatively straightforward in design. However, despite its rather tentative initial approach to the electric market – and the horrified reaction of its founder's son to the introduction of Gibson's solid-bodied instrument (see pages 52-53) – Gretsch quickly developed a flair for colorful finishes and extra gadgetry. This more adventurous approach could be seen in some of its "Chet Atkins" archtops (see pages 74-75), and was also apparent on the top-of-the-line White Falcon model, which made its first appearance in 1955. An unashamedly ostentatious guitar, with a retail price of $600, it boasted gold sparkle decoration, gold-plated metalwork, and bird and feather engravings on its pickguard and fingerboard

position markers. Its later versions incorporated additional features such as stereo circuitry and an ingenious mechanical string "muffler" mounted between the back pickup and the bridge (illustrated opposite).

Gretsch guitars were especially popular with country musicians and rockers, including Hank Garland, Duane Eddy, and the tragically short-lived Eddie Cochran. The company also had a following among several major jazz artists; its 1959 floating-pickup "Convertible" electric/acoustic was endorsed by Sal Salvador, former guitarist with the Stan Kenton Big Band, who had a long association with them.

A year before, Gretsch had celebrated 75 years in the instrument-making business by launching a pair of new electric archtops, the Anniversary (single pickup) and the twin pickup Double Anniversary. These models were fitted with the company's new "Filter'Tron" humbuckers (previous Gretsch electrics had used single-coil transducers manufactured by DeArmond) and, at under $200 each, were comparatively inexpensive guitars, "priced for promotional selling" as the company's publicity put it; they remain desirable collectors' items.

Left: Gretsch electric archtop, 1953. Confusingly, Gretsch used the "Synchromatic" headstock label for both acoustic and electric guitars in the early 1950s.

This model is especially unusual because of the position of its controls; Gretsch electrics of the period normally had three knobs on the lower treble bout and a fourth (master volume) near the cutaway.

(COURTESY LLOYD CHIATE, VOLTAGE GUITARS, HOLLYWOOD)

Left and bottom left: *Gretsch White Falcon, 1966. The original White Falcon, launched in 1955, had a single cutaway; this double-cutaway version appeared in the early 1960s. It is fitted with two "Filter'Tron" pickups, and its string mutes (the two black pads just above the bridge) are controlled by twin lever switches on either side of the tailpiece.*

(COURTESY LLOYD CHIATE, VOLTAGE GUITARS, HOLLYWOOD)

Below: *Gretsch Double Anniversary, 1961. This later example has "HiLo 'Tron" single-coil pickups instead of the original "Filter'Tron" humbuckers. The instrument has a master volume control, individual knobs for each pickup volume, and two switches – one to select and combine the pickups, the other to provide different tone settings.*

(COURTESY SAN DIEGO GUITARS)

Gretsch and Chet Atkins

*I*n 1954, Gretsch signed an endorsement deal with star Nashville guitarist Chet Atkins – a move that proved to be a vital factor in the company's subsequent success. Atkins (b.1924), a top session musician with a high popular profile thanks to his solo work and TV appearances, was also assistant to the Head of RCA in Nashville, and in 1957, after he became Chief of RCA's Country Division, his career and reputation reached new heights. However, by the mid-1950s he had already played on, arranged, and produced a string of hit records, and was helping to shape what came to be known as the Nashville Sound.

The earliest versions of the first Gretsch Chet Atkins guitar, the 6120, were not entirely to the endorsee's liking when he first tried them. As he explained in *The Gretsch Book* by Tony Bacon & Paul Day: "The [pickup] magnets pulled so strong on the strings that there was no sustain there, especially in the bass." Atkins also had reservations about the styling, which featured a longhorn headstock logo and "Western" fret markers (subsequently phased out). However, he soon started using the new model for recordings and live work; it carried his signature on the pickguard, and, as he acknowledged to Bacon and Day, "I was *thrilled* to have my name on a guitar like Les Paul had his name on a Gibson."

Gretsch was equally thrilled to have Atkins on board; his presence had an impressive effect on its sales, and in 1957 a second Chet Atkins guitar, the Country Gentleman, was launched. It had one highly unusual feature for an electric archtop: no soundholes. Atkins and Gretsch found that sealing the instrument's top helped to minimize acoustic feedback, and the f-holes on most models (including the one shown here) are simply painted on as a *trompe l'oeil* effect.

The Country Gentleman was followed a year later by a lower-price design, the Tennessean, which was originally fitted with a single pickup; all three instruments remained in production until the 1980s. A Chet Atkins model manufactured by Gibson, the SST, is also featured on pages 102-103.

Opposite page:

Gretsch Chet Atkins Hollow Body (Model 6120), 1959. The instrument's distinctive "amber red" finish was originally combined with a stylized black "G" painted onto its lower bass bout. This, like the Western-style decorations, was removed from later versions. The single-coil pickups whose magnets Chet Atkins complained about were subsequently replaced by Gretsch "Filter'Tron" humbuckers, which are fitted here.

Left and above, inset: Gretsch Chet Atkins Country Gentleman, 1965. The Country Gentleman has a 17-inch (43.2cm) body (an inch wider than the 6120). On this example, the pickguard does not have the Chet Atkins signature that appears on the other two guitars, though the model name is shown on the metal plate screwed to the headstock. Note the fake f-holes!

(COURTESY LLOYD CHIATE, VOLTAGE GUITARS, HOLLYWOOD)

Below: Gretsch Chet Atkins Tennessean, 1963. The first version of the Tennessean, which appeared in 1958, had just one humbucking pickup, but in the early 1960s two single-coil transducers were substituted. Like all the instruments here, it is fitted with a Bigsby vibrato carrying the Gretsch name – Chet Atkins' preferred choice of unit.

(COURTESY ROD & HANK'S, MEMPHIS)

SECTION THREE:
The Evolving Electric

The mid-1960s were turbulent times for the electric guitar industry, with takeovers at Fender and subsequently at Gibson, and the departure of Leo Fender and Ted McCarty from the companies they had led since the 1940s. These two famous figures left a vacuum that their more business-oriented successors found it hard to fill, and for a number of years, both Fender and Gibson seemed in serious danger of losing their way. Many of their new instruments were failing to appeal to players, and Fender suffered increasing complaints from customers about quality control and standards of construction.

Alongside this disenchantment with current models was a growing reverence among musicians for earlier, "vintage" designs, as well as a desire for guitars that offered extra performance and personalized features. Some leading rock and jazz performers chose to have their instruments tailor-made by pioneering companies such as Alembic in San Francisco. Others took a "customizing" approach, combining and modifying existing components to make hot-rodded hybrids like the "Superstrats" first created in the 1970s by (among others) Grover Jackson and Eddie Van Halen.

Gibson and Fender (both of which acquired new, forward-looking and quality-conscious management teams in the 1980s) eventually responded to players' requirements by opening their own custom shops, reissuing accurate, lovingly made replicas of older models, and offering fresh and exciting additions to their instrument ranges. They and other major U.S. firms also manufacture lower-priced ranges of their own under licence in Japan, China, Korea, or Taiwan; a move that provides effective competition against the flood of Far Eastern imports that once posed such a severe threat to their livelihood. These policies have led to a proliferation of high-quality instruments at every price level; as one of the United Kingdom's leading luthiers, Hugh Manson, observes: "There's probably never been a better time to buy a good guitar."

Fender Telecaster, 1967. This guitar is a fairly typical early "post-CBS" model with a maple fingerboard and new, bolder headstock decal.

(COURTESY ROD & HANK'S, MEMPHIS)

CHAPTER 4
A CHANGING CLIMATE
1965–1980

Fender's takeover by New York-based broadcasting and entertainment conglomerate CBS (Columbia Broadcasting System) was announced officially on January 5, 1965. For a total purchase price of $13,000,000, CBS had acquired the company's entire manufacturing and sales operation. Don Randall, formerly President of Fender Sales, became Vice-President and General Manager of the new Fender division of CBS; Leo Fender was given a research and development consultancy, but took no further part in running his old business, and did not retain an office at its Fullerton headquarters.

Leo had been in poor health during the previous year, but the precise reasons for his decision to sell remain uncertain, although he knew that his firm needed a substantial injection of capital. CBS was able to provide it, but also brought a "big business" approach to Fender management and product development, which was soon to prove damaging to the health and reputation of its new subsidiary.

Under the new régime, workmanship and quality control were sometimes markedly inferior; the term "pre-CBS" began to be used by players to differentiate instruments produced after 1965 from those made while Leo Fender himself was still in charge. Also, a number of post-CBS designs simply did not measure up to the company's previous high standards. In 1966, a disagreement over a line of transistorized amplifiers led to the resignation of Manufacturing Operations Director Forrest White, who felt they were not worthy of the Fender name; and less than three years later, Don Randall himself decided to leave.

However, the change of management did not have an immediate effect on Fender instruments. Early CBS Telecasters look and sound little different from their pre-1965 counterparts, and it was not until well after the takeover that any significant changes to the company's classic designs began to be made. In 1967, the Telecaster was rewired to remove its bass boost circuit and allow two-pickup operation (see pages 32-33), and, the following year, a "new" Telecaster variant, the Thinline, was launched. This combined a half hollowed-out body with the standard Tele pickup configuration, neck, and body shape, and remained in production until the late 1970s.

Below: Fender Telecaster Thinline, 1971. The Thinline retains the standard Tele shape, but its bass side has a hollow cavity and sports an f-hole. When the instrument was introduced in 1968, it was fitted with single-coil pickups; but from 1971 these were replaced by humbuckers (as shown here) designed by Seth Lover, who had left Gibson to work for Fender in 1967.

The Fender Telecaster Thinline remained in production until 1978.
(COURTESY DAVE PEABODY)

Left: *Fender Telecaster Custom, 1967. The Custom Tele, which first appeared in 1959, has a bound body and an attractive sunburst finish. "Blonde" (as on the Bigsby-equipped guitar opposite) remained the sole finish on Standard Telecasters until 1974.*

(COURTESY MARK KNOPFLER)

Left: *The vibrato unit of the Fender Telecaster designed by Paul Bigsby was a popular choice among many players, but was not originally intended to work with Fender guitars and required considerable modification before it could be used on them. From about 1966 CBS/Fender offered it as a factory-fitted extra on Telecasters.*

Right: *Fender Telecaster with Bigsby vibrato, 1966.*

(COURTESY REAL GUITARS, SAN FRANCISCO)

The New Fullerton Plant and the Post-CBS Stratocaster

By 1966, CBS-Fender had a new 120,000 sq. ft. (1,115m²)factory, built adjacent to their original premises in Fullerton, and providing the latest and best in manufacturing facilities. As plant manager Forrest White observed in his book *Fender: The Inside Story,* its pristine, dust-free environment and stylish office furnishings were "quite a departure from what we had been used to." (Conditions in the older buildings had been much more spartan – even Leo Fender's personal research and development area, used for crucial tests and experiments on amplifiers, pickups, and other components, had occupied only a single workbench in a vacant room.)

The extra space and capacity were badly needed now, as CBS-Fender was widening its areas of operation – becoming involved in semi-acoustic guitar production (see pages 82-83), banjo-making, electric organ building, and, as mentioned earlier, solid-state amplification. None of these new ventures had been prompted by Leo himself, and one of the few substantial ideas he offered the company during his five-year term as a consultant – an ingenious design for a guitar string bender – was rejected by CBS as uncommercial.

The Stratocasters coming off the new production lines at Fullerton had slightly larger and differently shaped headstocks than their pre-CBS counterparts. This apparently minor modification is felt by many players and collectors to spoil the instrument's looks – and, as many of them have commented, it was possibly done to permit the use of a larger name/model decal! (See photographs opposite.) Another cosmetic change took place after 1968, when Fender abandoned the use of three-coat nitro-cellulose finishes on its instrument bodies, substituting polyester, which is easier to apply during mass production. In his exhaustive guide to the Stratocaster, guitar expert A.R. Duchossoir explains that while the original nitro-cellulose process involved just three coats of lacquer, the high-gloss "thick-skin" method that replaced it covered the wood with up to 15 layers of polyester – not only changing the instrument's appearance, but giving it a radically different feel in the player's hands. "Thick-skin" finishes can be seen on both the 1969 Strats shown on these pages.

Below left: *Fender Stratocaster, 1969. Curiously, Leo Fender never registered his company's distinctive "Fender" and "letter F" trademarks – an omission that CBS corrected in 1967. As a result, both this blonde Strat and the blue model below display the ® symbol on their decals.*
(COURTESY ROOM 335, ROSE-MORRIS, LONDON)

All these Stratocasters feature the enlarged headstock introduced within a year of the CBS takeover. A smaller headstock design, similar to the original, appeared in 1981.

Left: *Fender Stratocaster, 1969. This elegant model has a sonic blue finish – the lightest shade of blue offered by Fender during this period. The 1969 list price for a custom color Strat was $367 – 5 percent greater than the cost of a "standard" instrument.*
(COURTESY STEPHEN STRACHAN; PHOTOGRAPHED AT VOLTAGE GUITARS, HOLLYWOOD)

Above and inset: *Fender Stratocaster, 1966. This example has a dakota red custom finish; dakota was Fender's medium red custom coloring, lighter than the popular "candy apple red" but darker than "fiesta." The enlarged, post-CBS headstock has a "transitional" decal; the "Fender" and "Stratocaster" lettering are smaller and less bold than on the other two instruments shown here.*
(COURTESY AMANDA'S TEXAS UNDERGROUND, NASHVILLE)

Fender in the Late 1960s and 1970s

Fender was certainly not short of new guitar models during the early CBS period. One of the first (and least successful) of these was the Marauder, a four-pickup solid launched in 1965 and available for less than a year. It was followed, in 1968, by the Bronco, a single-pickup, double-cutaway instrument whose body bore a close resemblance to the pre-CBS Mustang (illustrated on pages 48-49). Both steeds survived in the company catalog until the 1980s.

A more surprising departure for the company was its introduction of a number of acoustic and semi-acoustic guitars in the mid-1960s. In fact, Leo Fender himself had previously shown interest in this area, hiring Roger Rossmeisl (the designer of the classic Rickenbacker electro-acoustics – see pages 70-71) in 1962, and working with him over the next two years on a range of five acoustics – including even a nylon-strung classical model. Rossmeisl stayed on after Leo's departure, and was responsible for many of CBS-Fender's later flat-top acoustic and archtop electric guitars, including the Coronado, which debuted in 1966.

Coronados, along with several other post-CBS Fender instruments, were available for a time either in standard finishes or in five shades of "Wildwood" – a beechwood injected, while still growing, with special dyes that created distinctive colorings. Wildwood (not itself a Fender product; it had been developed in Scandanavia) was used on a number of the company's solid-body models, but was probably most effective on acoustic or semi-acoustic designs such as the Coronado II shown opposite.

The Coronados had considerable merits, but the guitar-purchasing public associated Fender too closely with solid electrics such as the Telecaster and Stratocaster to accept them. Sadly, the same fate was to befall Fender's most attractive and underrated semi-acoustic, the Starcaster, which dates from 1975. A thinline model, fitted, unusually for Fender, with humbucking pickups (the "Fender sound" is invariably associated with single-coil units, although humbuckers were available on a number of its post-CBS guitars), the Starcaster might have provided an effective challenge to some Gibson and Gretsch semi-acoustics. However, it never sold in large numbers, and was withdrawn in 1982.

Far left and inset: *Fender Coronado II Wildwood II, 1968. Wildwood finishes were available in a variety of colors; this one (number II) is green, gold, and brown. The Coronado was Fender's first semi-acoustic; designed by Roger Rossmeisl (formerly of Rickenbacker), it was made in one- and two-pickup configurations, and there was also a twelve-string version*
(COURTESY ROD & HANK'S, MEMPHIS)

Below left: *Fender Starcaster, c.1976. Unusually for a Fender, the Starcaster has five control knobs – individual volume and tone for each pickup, plus a master volume. The pickup selector switch on the upper treble bout is not the original component.*
(COURTESY JOHN FIRTH)

Lower right: *Fender Bronco, 1977. Like its two-pickup cousin, the Mustang, the Bronco was chiefly intended for the student market, at whom CBS-Fender also aimed new products such as the smaller, lighter transistorized amplifiers launched in 1967 despite the disapproval of many old Fender employees.*
(COURTESY ROD & HANK'S, MEMPHIS)

Gibson's "Modernistic" Guitars

*I*n the 1950s, Fender had shaken up the guitar-making establishment with its bold solid-body designs. Gibson had responded with the Les Paul, a highly effective instrument, but clearly the product of a maker with roots in traditional lutherie. For some critics, the Les Paul was simply not radical enough, as Ted McCarty, the firm's former President, admitted in an interview for "The Gibson" in 1996. "Other guitar makers [were saying] that Gibson was a fuddy duddy old company without a new idea in years. That information came back to me, so I said we would shake 'em up if that's what they thought." McCarty quickly commissioned sketches for some brand-new designs, and the resultant drawings and specifications were to form the basis for some of the wildest looking instruments in Gibson's history.

The most celebrated of these models, all of which had bodies made from African korina wood, was the Flying V, whose extraordinary shape derived from a tongue-in-cheek idea of McCarty himself. A few were produced in 1958, but the V was soon discontinued, although it was to make frequent reappearances in the Gibson catalog from the mid-1960s onwards. Its real fame came after its adoption by bluesman Albert King (1923–1992); later, it was a favorite with many hard rock and heavy metal players, notably Andy Powell of Wishbone Ash.

The second of McCarty's "modernistic" guitars (as they were described in company literature), the Explorer, had an angular body shape with dramatically extended upper treble and lower bass bouts, and shared the same electronics as the Flying V. Original examples of it are very rare, and no more than 40 1958-vintage examples are thought to have been built. The Explorer design then went out of production until 1975, when the model was reissued in a mahogany-bodied version.

The third guitar in the series, the Moderne, has a bizarre, myth-laden history. Its design was certainly blueprinted and patented in 1958, but despite persistent rumours to the contrary, was probably never actually produced at all! The version shown below is one of a limited edition of 500 Modernes issued by Gibson in 1982; the guitar had never been revived.

Below: The Gibson Flying V makes a wonderful visual impact, but its radical shape makes it extremely difficult to play while sitting down.
(COURTESY PAUL EVANS)

Right: Gibson Flying V, late 1970s. A reissue of Ted McCarty's wild design, which first appeared in 1958. Most later Flying Vs like this one are made from mahogany, not korina wood, and are fitted with conventional "stop" tailpieces instead of the V-shaped metal plates found on the originals.

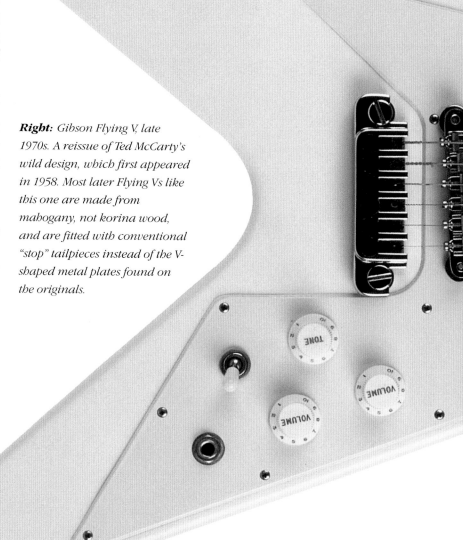

Right: Headstock of the Gibson Moderne "reissue."

Above: Gibson Moderne "reissue," 1982. No original 1958 Modernes have ever been discovered – although Ted McCarty suggests, in his interview for "The Gibson," that up to four prototypes may have been constructed for a trade show in New York.

The limited-edition replica of the Moderne was made using the original plans for the guitar; its body, like that of the original Flying V and Explorer, is made from African korina wood.

(COURTESY ROOM 335, ROSE-MORRIS, LONDON)

Above: The headstock of the Gibson Flying V.

The Gibson Firebirds

Gibson's "modernistic" guitars had proved too advanced for their time; but Ted McCarty continued his quest for a contemporary-looking solid-body model to provide serious competition for Fender. In the early 1960s, he decided to seek inspiration from a distinguished outsider: Ray Dietrich, a leading Detroit-based automobile designer famous for his work with Chrysler and Packard, who had never previously been involved with musical instruments. Dietrich was invited to submit sketches for a new-style guitar body, and his ideas were eventually realized as the Gibson Firebird.

The original Firebird featured a reverse body shape, with its treble wing or "horn" larger than the one on its opposite (bass) side, and a "six-tuners-in-a-row" headstock, of the type first adopted by Gibson on the ill-fated Explorer, oriented the "wrong" way round. The tuning machines themselves were banjo-type units with their buttons facing downwards, not sideways. The new guitar had a "neck-through-body" construction, and was made from mahogany; its pickups were the mini-humbuckers previously designed for Gibson's Epiphone line by Seth Lover. Four Firebird instruments, available in basic sunburst or, like their Fender competitors, in a

*Not only is the body of the Gibson Firebird VII no longer reversed; the headstock (**inset above**) is configured normally and the neck-through-body construction has been abandoned.*

Below left: *Gibson Firebird VII (reverse body), 1965. The three-pickup Firebird VII has a mahogany center section, with the instrument's two wings glued onto either side. Other models in the series, which was introduced in 1963, are fitted with single or paired mini-humbucking pickups. Among the optional finishes available to customers were kerry green, frost blue, or polaris white.*

(COURTESY LLOYD CHIATE, VOLTAGE GUITARS, HOLLYWOOD)

Above: *Gibson Firebird VII (non-reverse body), 1966.* (COURTESY LLOYD CHIATE, VOLTAGE GUITARS, HOLLYWOOD)

range of custom colors, were launched in 1963; the model name was suggested by Ray Dietrich, and he also contributed the bird sketch visible on the pickguards of the guitars illustrated here.

The Firebirds were competitively priced (from $189.50 to $445 for a top-of-the-line Firebird VII like the one illustrated here), and certainly lived up to the claims of Gibson's publicity, which described them as "revolutionary in shape, sound and colors." However, they met the same resistance as the Flying V and Explorer, and also provoked a complaint from Fender, who

claimed that the design infringed their patents. This was denied by Gibson, and no action was ever taken; but the dispute was probably a factor in Ted McCarty's decision, made during 1965, to modify the Firebirds' appearance and construction, and drop the reverse body shape. The line survived only four more years before being discontinued, but like several other "radical" Gibson solid-body models, Firebirds have grown in popularity since their initial appearance, and the company has produced numerous reissues and replicas of them in recent years.

Gibson in the Late 1960s and 1970s

The Firebirds were the last major new electric models introduced by Ted McCarty, who left Gibson in 1966 after 16 years as its President. Two years later, the company changed hands; its new owner was Norlin Industries, which derived its name from Maurice Berlin of CMI (Gibson's former owners) and Norton Stevens of ECL Industries, the incoming purchasers. The Norlin régime at Kalamazoo brought about some major changes in working practices, design, and marketing – focusing on high volume production in an increasingly competitive market, and transferring the construction of Epiphone instruments to the Far East, where manufacturing costs were much lower.

For some time, CMI had used Epiphone as a lower-cost "companion brand," and many Epi models were, to put it crudely, slightly downmarket copies of standard Gibson designs. However, on one occasion in the 1970s, this process was put into reverse, when a fine Epiphone instrument, the Howard Roberts Custom semi-acoustic (developed in collaboration with Roberts [b.1929], a distinguished jazz player), was reintroduced as a Gibson! The rebranded

guitar was launched in 1974, and is shown below; five years later, Gibson produced another Howard Roberts model, the Fusion, this can be seen on pages 104-105.

The late 1960s and 1970s also saw several additions to familiar Gibson lines. A few short-lived new SGs appeared, and after Les Paul renewed his endorsement deal with the company in 1967, there was a rash of new and reissued models bearing his name, some of them with special on-board electronics. Among these is the Les Paul Signature illustrated here – a thinline archtop bearing little family resemblance to regular solid-body Les Pauls, although its distinctive coloring is a nod towards the instrument's earliest "gold-top" version. The Signature has the low impedance pickup circuitry favored by Les himself since the late 1960s, and a three-position "vari-tone" switch.

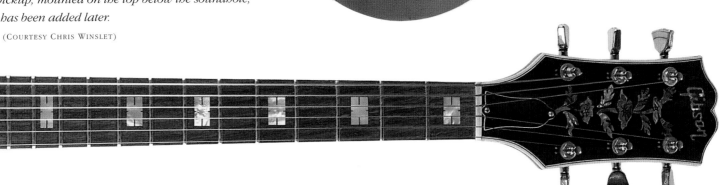

Below left: *Gibson Les Paul Signature, c.1974. The Signature was first produced in 1973; despite its hollow-body design, it retains a characteristic deep Les Paul-style cutaway on the right of the neck. Its low-impedance pickups are thought to offer greater clarity and superior frequency response; however, they require extra circuitry to make them compatible with standard high-impedance guitar amplifiers, and the Signature incorporates two separate outputs, offering low- and high-impedance signals.* (COURTESY ROD & HANK'S, MEMPHIS)

Below left: *Gibson Howard Roberts Custom, c.1975. This version of the Howard Roberts Custom is in a wine red finish. The "wandering vine" headstock **(opposite page, left)** decoration, a characteristic Epiphone feature, is "borrowed" from the original model. The instrument is 16 inches (40.6cm) wide; its second pickup, mounted on the top below the soundhole, has been added later.*

(COURTESY CHRIS WINSLET)

The third instrument on these pages is a more conventional gold-top: a Les Paul Deluxe dating from 1971. This attractive (and obviously heavily-played) guitar is fitted with Epiphone-style mini-humbuckers; their cream-colored mountings and the trapeze-shaped fingerboard inlays are among the guitar's many 1950s-like features.

This page, center right: *Gibson Les Paul Deluxe, 1971. The Deluxe was available in red or blue "sparkle" as well as in this distinctive gold finish. Its mini-humbucking pickups provide a less powerful, thinner sound than the full-size units found on 1960s Les Pauls. The model remained in the catalog until 1982.*

(COURTESY SAN DIEGO GUITARS)

Alembic – Realizing Musicians' Dreams

An "alembic" is defined in the dictionary as "anything that refines or purifies;" more specifically, it was the vessel in which medieval and Renaissance alchemists combined base metals as they sought to transmute them into gold. A different kind of alchemy is practiced at Alembic, Inc., of Santa Rosa, California, which produces fine instruments for some of the world's most outstanding performers. Its General Manager, Mica Wickersham, explains that the company name (with its distinctive trademark, shown above right), "has become for us a symbol of purity – and one of our primary goals is purity of sound."

Alembic was founded in 1969 by Mica's parents, Ron and Susan, who are still at the helm of the business. Ron, an electronics engineer, had a background in broadcasting, and subsequently became closely involved with the development of multi-track recording systems, while Susan was a successful artist. Their new company shared premises near San Francisco with the city's legendary rock group, the Grateful Dead, and was responsible for much of the band's sound technology – including its innovative PA system, and the "active" pickups used by bassist Phil Lesh, and guitarists Jerry Garcia and Bob Weir.

Below and opposite page, left: *Alembic 25th Anniversary Sterling bass, 1997. This limited-edition instrument (only 25 were made) commemorates 25 years of bass building at Alembic. (Users include the great jazz-rock player Stanley Clarke, who bought his first Alembic in 1972.) Susan Wickersham (who designs the body shapes of all Alembic instruments) was responsible for the selection of woods and other materials for the guitar.*

Its metal parts are sterling silver, its top and back are made from 15-year old Brazilian burl rosewood (highly prized by luthiers for its sound, and now a protected species), and the neck is maple and ebony.

(COURTESY ALEMBIC, INC.)

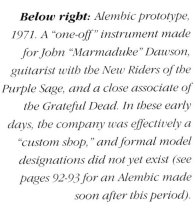

Below right: *Alembic prototype, 1971. A "one-off" instrument made for John "Marmaduke" Dawson, guitarist with the New Riders of the Purple Sage, and a close associate of the Grateful Dead. In these early days, the company was effectively a "custom shop," and formal model designations did not yet exist (see pages 92-93 for an Alembic made soon after this period).*

(COURTESY REAL GUITARS, SAN FRANCISCO)

In 1974, after several years combining electronics and instrument design with studio management and live recording work, Alembic decided to focus solely on making guitars, basses, and pickups. From the start, its instruments were strikingly different from those of more mainstream manufacturers. While standard electric guitar pickups are "voiced" to create a distinctive tone-color that cannot be substantially modified, Alembic transducers deliver a clean, high fidelity response that musicians then tailor to their needs by the use of active on-board filters, whose roll-off characteristics are carefully chosen to sound "natural" and musical. The resultant range of sonic possibilities gives players a uniquely versatile tool with which to realize their ideas. As Ron Wickersham puts it: "Rather than handing a musician something and saying, 'We have this great inspiration, and if you take our instrument, you'll be famous just like somebody else,' we do the opposite; the musician is free to come to us, and we don't try to talk him out of his dream."

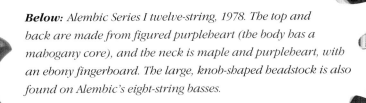

Below: *Alembic Series I twelve-string, 1978. The top and back are made from figured purpleheart (the body has a mahogany core), and the neck is maple and purpleheart, with an ebony fingerboard. The large, knob-shaped headstock is also found on Alembic's eight-string basses.*

(COURTESY ALEMBIC, INC.)

Guitars for Rock Stars

Speculation and myth often surround claims that particular instruments were once the property of famous players. However, there is no doubt about the provenance of the two models shown opposite, both of which are known to have belonged to major figures in the world of 1960s and 1970s rock. The Rickenbacker 360/12 is particularly significant: currently owned by Lloyd Chiate of Vintage Guitars in Hollywood, it was the guitar played by Jim (now Roger) McGuinn of The Byrds on the group's classic singles *Mr. Tambourine Man* and *Turn, Turn, Turn* (1965).

McGuinn (b.1942) first heard Rickenbacker twelve-strings on The Beatles' early records (see pages 52-53 and 70-71), and purchased this 360/12 in 1964, after seeing George Harrison using one in the movie *A Hard Day's Night.* The following year, The Byrds were formed (the band also included David Crosby and Chris Hillman), and their distinctive sound, strongly featuring McGuinn's new twelve-string, quickly brought them critical and commercial success on both sides of the Atlantic.

In 1966, the 360 was returned to Rickenbacker for some modifications; surviving paperwork shows that an extra pickup, a new nut, and a "pickguard with special wiring" were fitted. Roger McGuinn was photographed using the instrument onstage before and after these changes; he subsequently bought several other Rickenbackers, but this model was the first and most famous of his twelve-strings.

The Alembic Series II also illustrated here dates from 1972, and was custom-made for English rock musician Greg Lake (b.1948) – best known as a bassist, but also an accomplished six-string player. Lake first came to fame with King Crimson in 1969, before becoming a member of the hugely successful progressive rock trio Emerson, Lake and Palmer (ELP). The body of his Alembic has an African zebrawood top and back with a maple core; the front and back veneers on the headstock are coco bolo, and the "through" neck is made from layers of maple, purpleheart, and cherry wood. The instrument features Ron Wickersham's active pickup circuitry (see pages 90-91), and the side of its ebony fingerboard is fitted with illuminating LEDs. The beautiful mother-of-pearl inlays are the work of Ron's wife Susan.

Left: *Rickenbacker 360/12, 1964. The 360 is "officially" a two-pickup instrument; Roger McGuinn's guitar acquired its extra pickup and additional circuitry during a factory refit in 1966. Like all Deluxe Rickenbackers, it has triangular fret markers and a bound body. Note the ingenious "compact" headstock design, which disguises the six extra tuning machines by fitting them with their tuner buttons facing downwards.*

Above top: *Alembic Series II, 1972. When this guitar was made for rock star Greg Lake, model names had only just been introduced at Alembic, and there was considerable variation between individual instruments. Lake's Series II is slightly thicker than more recent examples, and its electronic circuitry is mounted on the right of its body (later Alembics have their electronics split between both body halves). It has recently been given a new finish, which has been carefully tinted to match the original coloring.*
Inset pictures: *Details of the Alembic Series II's headstock and neck inlays.*

Unusual Electrics

The first guitar shown here dates from 1968, and its "cresting wave" double cutaway, single pickup, overall shape and finish are identical to those on a Rickenbacker Combo 425. However, it carries the Electro label; Electro String was, of course, Rickenbacker's original manufacturing company, and for some years, the Electro marque was retained for instruments sold directly to teaching studios, usually as part of a beginner's "outfit" that also included an amplifier and case. As John C. Hall, Rickenbacker's Chairman and CEO, explains: "Electro guitars were made in the same factory as Rickenbackers, and a lot of the models are the same [as] Rickenbacker models – except that they were not buffed out and polished to the same degree, in order to keep the cost down." Occasionally, though, an Electro instrument would be out-of-stock when required; then an equivalent, finely polished Rickenbacker, like the one opposite, would have its original logo replaced, and be sent out as an Electro.

C.F. Martin & Company, of Nazareth, Pennsylvania, is justly famous for its fine flat-top acoustic guitars; however, the firm's strong association with this particular type of instrument has meant that its occasional forays into archtop, electric, and bass production have never been especially successful. The Martin EM-18 illustrated opposite was part of a range of solid-body guitars introduced in 1979, which remained in the catalog for only four years. Significantly, its headstock (whose scrolled shape is reminiscent of the earliest nineteenth century Martin acoustics) bears the company's initials rather than its full name. It is an attractive and versatile instrument, with two humbucking pickups, coil selector and phase switches, and a maple body with walnut laminates. The E series also featured some models with active electronics.

The third guitar on these pages is a Kapa Continental – a copy of Fender's Jazzmaster/Jaguar design, but produced by a homegrown American company, rather than one of the Far Eastern competitors that were soon to have such a devastating effect on U.S. manufacturers. Kapa, based in Maryland, was in business between 1966 to 1970; it also produced a twelve-string version of the Continental, fitted, like the model shown here, with a vibrato unit.

Right and below: *Electro ES-17, 1968. The superb sheen on this Fireglo-colored instrument betrays its origins as a relabelled Rickenbacker. John C. Hall, the company's CEO, points out that the "conversion" process could also work the other way: "Through the years, many people have taken Electro guitars, buffed them out, and put Rickenbacker nameplates on them – but [the instruments] didn't leave the factory as Rickenbackers".*
(COURTESY RICKENBACKER INTERNATIONAL CORPORATION)

Right: *Kapa Continental, late 1960s. This model has an unusual blue-green finish. Its body shape and (especially) its vibrato unit are strongly reminiscent of the Fender Jazzmaster and Jaguar – although, unlike them, the Kapa is fitted with a zero fret.*
(Courtesy Amanda's Texas Underground, Nashville)

Right: *CFM EM-18, c.1980. Martin's E series included two other six-string guitars, as well as a pair of basses. The instrument shown here has a mahogany neck and a rosewood fingerboard; its pickups and "Badass" bridge (designed to improve sustain) were bought in from other manufacturers.*
(Courtesy Amanda's Texas Underground, Nashville)

CHAPTER 5
INNOVATION AND TRADITION – 1980 TO THE PRESENT

*L*eo Fender's departure, in 1965, from the company that bore his name did little to dampen his subsequent creativity. However, the terms of his consultancy contract with CBS meant that he could do no guitar design work on his own account until 1970, and it was two more years before he launched his next business venture, Tri-Sonics, later renamed Music Man. Leo's partners in the firm were both ex-Fender employees: former General Manager Forrest White; and Tom Walker, who had been a key figure in Fender sales. Another Fender "old-timer," George Fullerton, came to work for Music Man in 1974.

Leo Fender could probably have had considerable success by turning out replicas of his classic Telecasters and Stratocasters at Music Man, but he had no intention of retreading old ground. As George Fullerton explained in a 1991 *Vintage Guitar* magazine interview with Willie G. Moseley, "What Leo tried to do…was to make [guitars] that didn't look like the legendary instruments he'd designed at Fender, and he wanted these newer brands to be *improvements* on his earlier designs. In a lot of ways, he had his work cut out for him, but he felt like his later designs were the best he'd ever done." New features on Music Man guitars

Below: Music Man Sabre I, late 1970s. This model, which first appeared in 1978, features two humbucking pickups. Its body outline is slightly reminiscent of a Stratocaster's, but there is no vibrato unit.

Music Man guitars, basses, and amplifiers were actually manufactured by CLF Research, the Fullerton-based company set up by Leo Fender after the CBS takeover.

(COURTESY ROD & HANK'S, MEMPHIS)

Leo Fender's office, G & L Musical Instruments, Fullerton, California. The office and desk have been preserved exactly as Leo Fender left them on the day before his death. His test equipment, including an oscilloscope and multimeter (with a bottle of Listerene antiseptic mouthwash beside it) is within easy reach. On the back wall behind the chair is another bench holding the guitars he was working on, and a door leading to a small inner room.

(COURTESY G & L MUSICAL INSTRUMENTS)

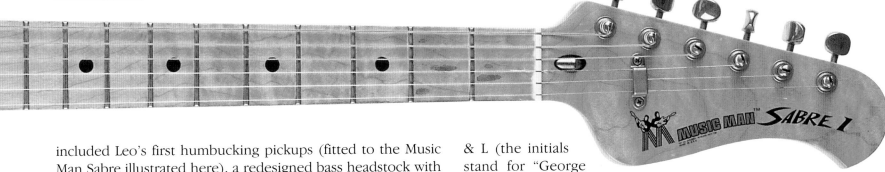

included Leo's first humbucking pickups (fitted to the Music Man Sabre illustrated here), a redesigned bass headstock with one tuning machine positioned opposite the other three, and active electronics similar to those pioneered by Alembic a few years earlier.

Despite the high quality of these instruments, Music Man's success was limited – due, in part, to growing disagreements between the three principal shareholders. In 1980, Fender and Fullerton left to set up another company, G & L (the initials stand for "George and Leo"). They were joined by Dale Hyatt, whose association with Leo dated back to 1946; he became G & L's Director of Marketing and Distribution.

The new venture saw the last flowering of Leo Fender's genius for guitar design; he worked at G & L until his death in 1991, developing many of his ideas at the workbench shown on this page.

Leo Fender, George Fullerton, and G & L

G & L maintains Leo Fender's innovative approach to guitar design, as well as the hands-on production methods he always favored. Johnny McLaren, the current Plant Manager, explains that Leo "was fascinated by the mechanics of the manufacturing side," and always keen to purchase the finest and most advanced equipment for guitar making. Since the company's formation in 1980, as many of its components as possible have been produced at its own factory in Fullerton, California; those that have to be bought in come from manufacturers with established traditions of excellence. For example, the cloth-wrapped wire used in some instruments is made by Gavitt Wire & Cable of Massachusetts, which once supplied pioneering automobile builder Henry Ford.

G & L also draws more direct inspiration from its founders. George Fullerton, Leo Fender's partner in the company, lives nearby, and continues to work as a consultant, and Leo's own drawings and notes still provide Johnny McLaren with valuable guidance. "Every time we've had problems here I can go back to Leo's file cabinet and get the exact numbers. Everything's there – it's picture perfect."

George and Leo's approaches to guitar making were complementary. Leo could not play the instrument, although he loved music; while George, an accomplished performer,

often contributed to the more artistic aspects of a design. Leo excelled at the mechanical and engineering sides, and never lost his enthusiasm for developing fresh ideas. John C. McLaren, Johnny McLaren's father, whose company, BBE Sound, now owns G & L, paints a vivid picture of Leo on holiday with his second wife, Phyllis: "To please [her] he went on these cruises. They'd be invited to sit at the captain's table…and Leo'd be sitting there drawing new pickups. Then, at the next port, he'd fax them back to George Fullerton!"

One such design, the "Magnetic Field" pickup, is featured on the ASAT Junior illustrated opposite. Another important innovation from Leo Fender's G & L years is the Dual Fulcrum tremolo fitted to two of the instruments shown here. Even the Legacy model, produced posthumously as a tribute to Leo's life and achievements, is largely based on his own ideas and drawings.

Below: The headstock of the G & L Legacy, 1998.

Right: G & L ASAT Junior (limited edition), 1998. The ASAT (named after the U.S. Air Force's Anti-Satellite Missile) has an overall shape similar to a Telecaster's. This model, one of a limited edition of 250, has hollow side chambers and a solid center. Its body and neck are mahogany, and its fingerboard ebony. The Magnetic Field pickups, with their fully adjustable pole pieces, provide a warm, rich sound and a high electrical output.

Above: *G & L Legacy, 1998. The Legacy has three G & L Alnico V single-coil pickups in a Stratocaster-type configuration, with a five-way selector switch. The guitar's body is alder, and the neck is maple. Leo Fender's patented Dual Fulcrum tremolo features two pivoting points anchored into brass inserts in the instrument's body. It gives a smoother feel than earlier units, and permits notes to be bent up as well as down.*

Above left: *G & L S.500, 1998. This example is finished in "cherry burst." It has a hard rock maple neck (with rosewood fingerboard) and a body of alder. Like the Legacy, it is fitted with a Dual Fulcrum tremolo unit, but its "whammy bar" has been removed for this photograph.*

Gibson in the Early 1980s

he 1970s had been a confusing and increasingly troubled period for Gibson. Its guitars were never short of exposure: in fact, leading performers on both sides of the Atlantic were helping to make the Les Paul one of the dominant instruments of contemporary rock. Yet the models favored by these players often dated from the 1950s, and more recent Les Pauls, despite the variety of styles they appeared in, were judged by some musicians to be inferior to their predecessors in sound, feel, and appearance.

Many other Gibson solid bodies were also launched during the decade, but few seemed to catch on, or retain their place in the catalog for any length of time. Meanwhile, at the lower end of the market, cheap and increasingly proficient Far Eastern copies of Gibson's classic designs (and, of course, Fender's Telecasters and Stratocasters) were successfully circumventing the patent laws and doing substantial damage to the original manufacturers' worldwide sales.

In 1974, Norlin, Gibson's parent company, moved the bulk of its electric guitar production from Kalamazoo, Michigan (where the firm had been based since it was founded in 1902) to a new plant in Nashville, Tennessee. Only acoustic and some top range semi-acoustic Gibson designs continued to be made at Kalamazoo. Ten years later, the original factory was closed permanently, and all instrument manufacture transferred to Nashville. The idea behind these changes was to rationalize and reduce costs, but difficulties and poor sales continued, and in 1985, Gibson was put up for sale. Like CBS, which disposed of Fender during the same period (see pages 108-109), Norlin clearly felt that the guitar building business held no future for it; and there were plenty of industry pundits and dealers who believed that Gibson itself might soon cease to exist.

However, the following year, Gibson was bought by a new management partnership headed by Henry Juszkiewicz, who has been its President ever since. His shrewd and capable management has succeeded in re-establishing the company at the forefront of the musical instrument business, and some of its outstanding current designs, displaying a fine blend of tradition and innovation, are featured on the next four pages.

Above: *Gibson Sonex 180 Deluxe, 1981. The Sonex line comprised three instruments, all with the same body shape, but offering a variety of pickup configurations and finishes. This is the most basic model, with two humbucking pickups and standard, passive circuitry*

Headstock, Gibson Les Paul Custom.

Below left: Gibson Les Paul Standard, 1989. An example of Gibson's output soon after its takeover by the new management team. This model is a very attractive reissue of a 1958-style Les Paul Standard, with a "vintage sunburst" finish

The model has a maple top and a mahogany body, and its trapeze-style fingerboard inlays closely match those of the original.

(COURTESY MARK KNOPFLER)

Above: The Sonex 180 Deluxe's body is made of Masonite, the hardboard material also used by Nathan Daniel on his Danelectro guitars (see pages 50-51). The model was manufactured for only three years, between 1981–84. (COURTESY ROD & HANK'S, MEMPHIS)

Left: Gibson Les Paul Custom, 1982. The Custom was one of the first of the Les Paul models to be reissued in 1968. The new version was fitted with only two humbucking pickups, but a third was frequently available as an option. This model is in the original ebony finish that gave the instrument its nickname "Black Beauty." (COURTESY ROD & HANK'S, MEMPHIS)

Gibson – Under New Management

*I*n the years immediately following their takeover, Henry Juszkiewicz and his team focused on producing and marketing Gibson's classic models, and the company's current catalog includes SGs, Les Pauls, 335s, and many other well-established instruments. There are also Custom and Historical ranges, and a small number of highly decorated Art Guitars – among them an Elvis Presley Super 400, and a special version of B.B. King's ES-355, "Lucille," made to celebrate the great bluesman's 70th birthday (see pages 104-105 for a standard "Lucille").

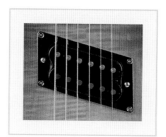

More recently, though, Gibson has been developing some impressive new designs – notably the Hawk Series, launched in 1993 with the three-pickup Nighthawk model. Designed by J.T. Riboloff, the company's Head of Research and Development, this instrument offers a remarkably wide range of sounds, thanks largely to its coil-tap switch, which doubles as a tone control knob. When this is pulled up, the guitar's neck and bridge humbuckers are converted to single-coil operation, providing a thinner, Stratocaster-like timbre that can be quickly changed back to a warmer, twin-coil tone as necessary. The Hawk family includes various different versions of the Nighthawk, as well as the twin-pickup BluesHawk, which appeared in 1995.

Among the many leading players currently associated with Gibson is Chet Atkins, who first collaborated with the company in 1982 to produce his innovative nylon-strung Standard CE (Classical Electric) – designed for fingerstyle playing without the risk of acoustic feedback. The relationship has continued to flourish under the new management (at one time, Chet and Henry Juszkiewicz had houses in the same Nashville street), and Gibson now manufactures its own versions of the Chet Atkins Country Gentleman and Tennessean archtops, originally developed and made by Gretsch (see pages 74-75). The model shown here is the SST – a steel-strung adaptation of Atkins' CE.

The third instrument on these pages, a double-cutaway LPS, revives the body outline found on the "intermediate" 1959–1961 style Les Paul featured on pages 42-43 – although its electronics have been updated, and its "tangerineburst" finish gives it a strikingly contemporary look. The model is also available in lemonburst, blackburst, and a range of solid colors.

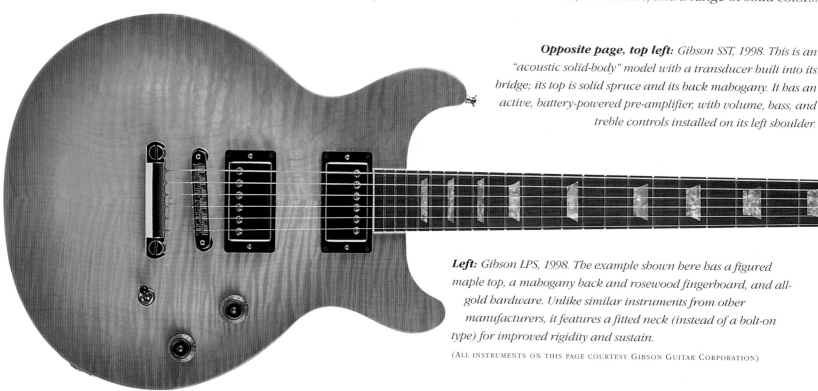

Opposite page, top left: *Gibson SST, 1998. This is an "acoustic solid-body" model with a transducer built into its bridge; its top is solid spruce and its back mahogany. It has an active, battery-powered pre-amplifier, with volume, bass, and treble controls installed on its left shoulder.*

Left: *Gibson LPS, 1998. The example shown here has a figured maple top, a mahogany back and rosewood fingerboard, and all-gold hardware. Unlike similar instruments from other manufacturers, it features a fitted neck (instead of a bolt-on type) for improved rigidity and sustain.*

(ALL INSTRUMENTS ON THIS PAGE COURTESY GIBSON GUITAR CORPORATION)

The Nighthawk's shape is slightly reminiscent of the Les Paul's, but with a wider body, deeper cutaway and an extended scale length.

Below: *Gibson Nighthawk DSNH, 1998. This sunburst-finish Nighthawk has two Gibson M-Series humbuckers in the neck and bridge positions (the bridge pickup is slanted* **opposite page, inset***) and a high-output single-coil transducer in the middle. There is a five-position pickup selector switch mounted below the volume and tone/coil-tap controls.*

The Jimmy Page Les Paul, "Lucille," and the Howard Roberts Fusion

One of the key figures behind the popularity of the Gibson Les Paul over the last 30 years is Led Zeppelin guitarist Jimmy Page – a virtuoso player with precise and demanding requirements for his instruments. When Gibson collaborated with Page to produce a Signature Model Les Paul, the new design was based on the musician's own customized 1959 LP Standard, and incorporated a number of special features. The company's Quality Control Supervisor, Francis Johns, explains that Page "wanted to try and achieve a guitar that felt like it had [already] been played, and was 'broken in.' The neck is unique: it's actually thinner in the center than it is at the top – Jimmy Page shaves his own guitars down to get this feel." The electronics are also unusual: the two humbucking pickups were specially designed for the instrument (the bridge unit is the highest output transducer Gibson has ever made), and the control circuitry offers coil-tapping, phasing, and series/parallel switching – as described in the caption. The Jimmy Page Les Paul is currently Gibson's most expensive production model; Page has given permission for only 2,200 instruments to be built.

Below: Gibson Jimmy Page Les Paul, 1998. This special model has a bookmatched figured maple top, gold hardware, and an elegant "light honeyburst" finish – but its sophisticated electronics are not so easily visible.

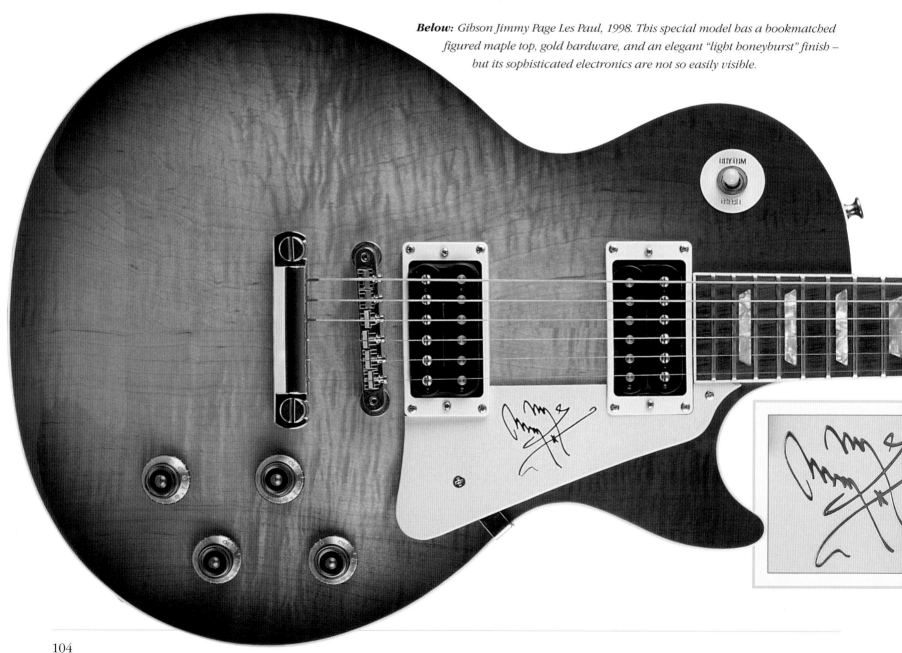

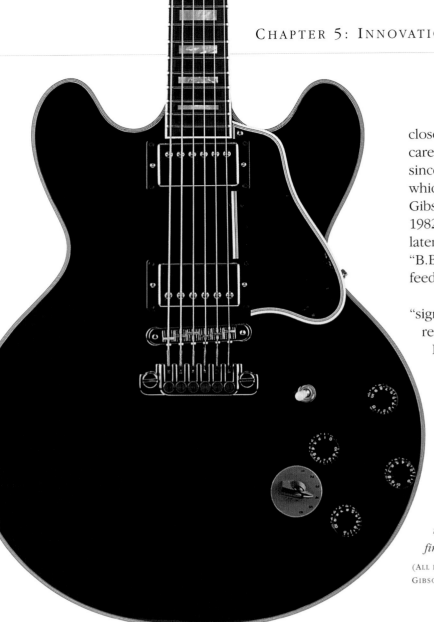

Bluesman B.B. King (b.1925) is another great guitarist closely associated with a specific Gibson model. Early in his career, King played a Fender Telecaster or a Gibson ES-5, but since the early 1960s he has used a succession of ES-355s, all of which have had the same famous nickname, "Lucille." In 1980, Gibson introduced a production "B.B. King" model, and since 1982, King has officially endorsed the instrument, which was later renamed "B.B. King Lucille." Unlike the original 355, the "B.B. King" has no f-holes; the sealed top helps to avoid feedback at high playing volumes.

Jazz musician Howard Roberts (1929–1992) had his first "signature" guitar made by Epiphone in 1965; later this was reissued under the Gibson marque (see pages 88-89). A new Howard Roberts model, the Fusion, appeared in 1980; it is a semi-solid design with a laminated maple body and neck and two humbucking pickups. Its distinctive "six-finger" tailpiece was added in 1990.

Left: *Gibson B.B. King Lucille, 1998. "Lucille," like her close relation, the ES-355, has stereo circuitry (the output from each pickup can be sent to a separate channel or amplifier) and a six-position rotary "Varitone" switch, visible just left of the volume and tone controls, which provides a selection of pre-set sounds. The instrument's body is laminated maple, with a solid center block; the fingerboard inlays are pearl.*

(ALL INSTRUMENTS ON THESE PAGES COURTESY GIBSON GUITAR CORPORATION)

*Each of the four control knobs on the Jimmy Page Les Paul **(above left)** can be pulled up to obtain additional effects: the tone control for the "rhythm" (neck) pickup switches the circuitry into series or parallel, while the other knobs offer coil tapping for each pickup, and put the two transducers in or out of phase with each other. Jimmy Page's signature **(left)** can be seen on the pickguard.*

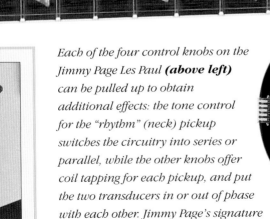

Left: *Gibson Howard Roberts Fusion, 1998. The "Fusion" has a number of unique features – including its unusually positioned volume and tone controls, its reshaped cutaway, and the distinctive tailpiece, which permits the player to adjust the angles of individual strings via the six rotary controls at its base. This unit, used in conjunction with the instrument's standard Gibson "Tune-O-Matic" bridge, allows a remarkable degree of control over string height, intonation, and position.*

Made In Kalamazoo –
The Heritage Range

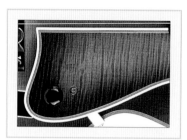

Gibson's departure from Kalamazoo, Michigan, in 1984 did not end the long history of guitar making there. A number of the company's employees decided to resign rather than make the 500-mile (800km) move to Nashville, and three senior ex-staffers – plant manager Jim Deurloo, plant superintendent Marv Lamb, and J.P. Moats (who had been in charge of wood purchasing, repairs, and custom orders) – made plans to continue fretted instrument construction in the town. Together with former Gibson accountant Bill Paige, they acquired premises and machinery from their previous employers, and set up their own business, Heritage Guitars Inc., in April 1985.

The firm's workforce was drawn from ex-Gibson craftsmen who, like the four founder/owners, had chosen to remain in Kalamazoo. Their collective skill and experience is reflected in the superb quality of Heritage's output, which includes electric and acoustic guitars as well as mandolins and banjos. The company is steeped in the Gibson/Kalamazoo tradition: its headstock logo, "The Heritage," is an echo of "The Gibson" trademark used on its predecessor's pre-war instruments; and a number of its models are strongly influenced by classic Gibson designs. However, Heritage instruments such as the "signature" guitars developed in collaboration with leading players like Johnny Smith, Roy Clark, and Alvin Lee invariably offer significant new refinements. The "Alvin Lee" has an ES-335-like body combined with a special three-pickup system, featuring two humbuckers and a single-coil transducer; while the "Johnny Smith," a reworking of the jazzman's classic electric/acoustic "floating-pickup" design (see pages 66-67) has delighted its creator, who personally signs every example.

All Heritage's full-body semi-acoustics, including the "Sweet 16" illustrated opposite, are fitted with solid wood tops (many post-war Gibson semis are made with laminates); and a wide variety of custom options is available across the company's entire range – from personalized inlays and special finishes to alternative pickups by EMG or Seymour Duncan. This combination of

expert craftsmanship and extensive customer choice – at highly competitive prices – has already brought Heritage considerable prestige, and after less than 15 years in business, it seems likely to succeed in its stated aim of creating "the collectible guitar of tomorrow."

Below: *Heritage Prospect Standard, 1998. The Prospect, introduced in 1991, is a 15-inch (38.1cm) semi-hollow design with a laminated curly maple top and back, and a mahogany neck. The instrument has a body depth of 1 1/2 inches (3.8cm), and is fitted with two humbucking pickups. It is available in three standard colors, almond sunburst (as shown here), antique sunburst, or natural.*

Right: Heritage H155, 1998. Like the other models in Heritage's H150 series, the H155 has a solid, carved body with a maple top, and two humbucking pickups.

Right: Heritage H155 headstock. The guitar's cutaway shape and pickguard design **(above)** are subtly different from those on the instrument that inspired it, the Gibson Les Paul. The guitar is finished in opaque blue.
(ALL INSTRUMENTS ON THESE PAGES COURTESY BARNES & MULLINS LTD.)

Above right: Heritage Sweet 16, 1998. As suggested by its name, this is a 16-inch (40.6cm) wide model – a genuine "semi-acoustic," with a depth of 2¾ inches (7cm). The pickguard carries the volume control **(opposite page, inset)** and supports the "floating" pickup, which does not touch the solid spruce top. (Pickups installed directly onto the top inevitably compromise an instrument's acoustic sound.) The back and sides of the guitar are made from curly maple, and the inlays on the headstock and ebony fingerboard are mother-of-pearl.

Fender in the 1980s and 1990s

The year 1980 marked the fifteenth anniversary of CBS's takeover of Fender, and as the decade began, its managers were faced with serious difficulties. The overall economic climate was bleak, Far Eastern imports were damaging sales, and substantial investment was needed to update tools and machinery. The company's reputation as a manufacturer of high quality instruments was also suffering – a situation exacerbated by a sometimes-exaggerated reverence for "pre-CBS" Fenders among many players. Such attitudes may not always have been fair, but it was a fact of life that while "an older [Fender] guitar was not necessarily better, most of the better guitars were old," as Richard R. Smith comments in his book *Fender: The Sound Heard 'Round the World.*

The following year, CBS made a serious effort to solve Fender's problems, hiring two senior executives from Yamaha's U.S. musical instruments division, John C. McLaren and William Schultz, to lead a new management team. They made substantial progress, replacing worn-out plant at the Fullerton factory, bringing in new models, and – in a radical and far-sighted move – launching a range of lower-priced Japanese-made Fender guitars. These included "reissues" of classic older designs, and were initially sold only in Japan and Europe; however, they soon appeared in the U.S. as well, giving a generation of impecunious young American players its first chance to own a "real" Strat or Tele.

Despite these achievements, however, CBS eventually decided to withdraw from the guitar industry. In 1985, it sold Fender to a consortium headed by Bill Schultz – who, like his former colleague John McLaren (now closely involved with G & L – see pages 98-99) was highly regarded by Fender personnel. In *Fender: The Inside Story,* Forrest White quotes company veteran Freddie Tavares as saying that "he thought Bill was the one who could restore [the firm] to its former position as king of the hill." Tavares' faith was justified; Fender has prospered under Schultz's leadership, and the proof of its renaissance lies in the range of excellent instruments it now produces – from the fine guitars made at its new factory and Custom Shop in Corona, California, to the cheaper models manufactured in Mexico and Asia.

Below left and right: Fender Telecaster Custom (made in Japan), c.1985. The Telecaster Custom made its first appearance in 1959; this reissued version was manufactured for Fender in Japan, and sold at a lower price than U.S.-made Fender instruments. Like the 1959 model, it has a sunburst finish, a bound top and back, and a rosewood fingerboard. The Schecter bridge unit, with its six individual saddles, is not original. (COURTESY NICK FREETH)

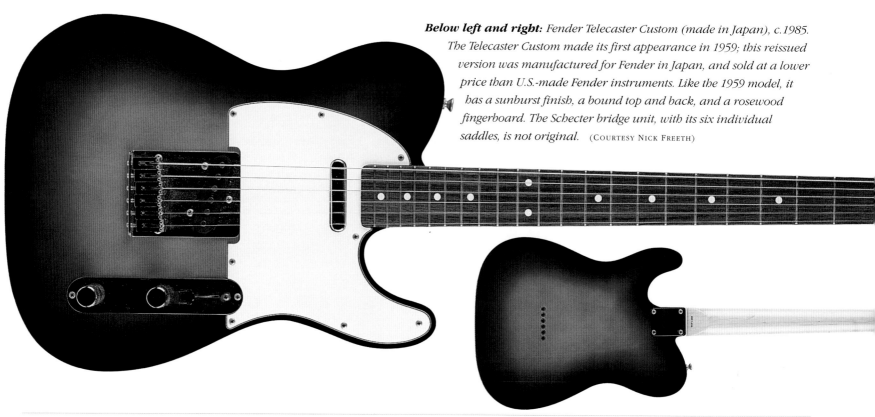

Above: *Fender 40th Anniversary Stratocaster, 1994. The Stratocaster, launched in 1954, is one of the most popular of all electric guitar designs – and certainly the most imitated. This "special edition" commemorative model, made at Fender's U.S. factory, features a "40th Anniversary" decal* **(opposite page, inset)** *on its headstock, and an appropriate slogan* **(right, inset)** *on its neck plate!*
(COURTESY AMANDA'S TEXAS UNDERGROUND, NASHVILLE)

Far right: *Fender "The Strat," 1980. This model was an attempt by CBS/Fender to regain some lost ground with players and collectors. It has gold hardware, its headstock – finished in candy-apple red, like the body – is smaller than previous CBS designs (compare it with the 1969 Strat on pages 80-81), and the neck is attached* to the instrument with four bolts, abandoning the less stable three-bolt system introduced in the early 1970s. "The Strat" was launched at the NAMM (National Association of Music Merchants) show in 1980, and remained in the catalog for three years.
(COURTESY AMANDA'S TEXAS UNDERGROUND, NASHVILLE)

Reworking The Classics

Telecasters and Stratocasters are now firmly established as classic guitars, but the profiles of some other Fender models are more dependent on particular musical trends, or identification with specific players. The Mustang, for example, was introduced in 1964 as a student instrument, but underwent a change of image after its adoption by Nirvana frontman Kurt Cobain (1967–1994). Cobain also admired the Fender Jaguar, and when he collaborated on a personalized guitar with the company's Custom Shop luthier Larry Brooks, he combined cut-up photographs of the two models to create a hybrid – naming it, appropriately, the Jag-Stang, and using the first version on Nirvana's 1993 tour dates. As Cobain explained in Fender's *Frontline* magazine, the Jag-Stang represents his attempt "to find the perfect mix of everything I was looking for." A second example was completed shortly before his death, and Fender subsequently obtained the agreement of his estate to manufacture the instrument, which is shown opposite.

Kurt Cobain's desire to "tailor" a guitar to his tastes and needs is nothing new. In the 1970s, Schecter Guitar Research of Los Angeles was already producing high quality replacement parts (including alternative pickups, bridges, vibrato units,and other hardware) for standard instruments like Strats and Teles. The company also operates a highly regarded Custom Shop service, which can build almost any combination of neck, body shape, and electronics to players' exact specifications. The Schecter "Telecaster" seen opposite was made for Mark Knopfler in 1984. It has been featured on many of his recordings, notably the classic Dire Straits number *Walk of Life*; and he invariably uses it when he plays the song live onstage.

The third model illustrated here is one of Rickenbacker's limited edition Artist series, the 355/12JL, commemorating John Lennon's close association with the company's instruments. It differs in some respects from the guitar actually used by Lennon with The Beatles – he played a ¾ size model 325, fitted with a vibrato unit – but features Lennon's signature and one of his cartoons on its pickguard, and is a fitting tribute to a musician who played a key role in popularizing Rickenbacker's classic designs.

Left: *Rickenbacker 355/12JL, late 1980s. A limited edition guitar featuring reproductions of John Lennon's distinctive artwork and signature **(right, inset)**. It is one of Rickenbacker's full-size "Thin Hollow Body" instruments, with a 15¼-inch (38.7cm) body width (Lennon's ³/₄ size 325 was only 12 ³/₄ inches [32.4cm] wide) and three pickups. The "355" serial number denotes a vibrato model, although one was not fitted to this special instrument. Unlike "Deluxe" Rickenbackers, the fingerboard has position dots, not "triangle" inlays, and the neck and body are unbound.*

(COURTESY RICKENBACKER INTERNATIONAL CORPORATION)

Right: *Schecter Custom "Telecaster," 1984. By the mid-1980s, a number of players were using Telecaster- and Stratocaster-style body shapes as the basis for customized guitars; Schecter is a leading maker of this type of instrument.*

Right: *Fender Jag-Stang, 1997 (left-hand model). This example, made by Fender Japan, is finished in sonic blue (like the second of the two Custom Shop Jag-Stangs made for Cobain himself – the other was red). It has a humbucking pickup at the bridge, and a single-coil unit in the neck position. The vibrato tailpiece and bridge are very similar to the Mustang's; the Jaguar influence can be seen in the shape of the bass (right) side of the body.*

(COURTESY AMANDA'S TEXAS UNDERGROUND, NASHVILLE)

*Special features and refinements on this hand-made Schecter "Telecaster" **(left)** include special pickups and an improved, fully-adjustable bridge assembly (also fitted to the Japanese Telecaster shown on page 108).*

(COURTESY MARK KNOPFLER)

Charvel, Grover Jackson and the "Soloist"

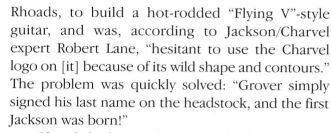

During the late 1970s, a new generation of virtuoso American guitarists was beginning to emerge. It included Eddie Van Halen (b.1957), born in Holland but brought up in California, who gave his surname to the powerful rock band he formed in 1973 with his brother Alex. Van Halen's debut LP appeared five years later, and Eddie quickly gained a reputation as a lightning-fast, intensely dramatic soloist who demanded the utmost from his instrument. Unsurprisingly, he and artists like him found basic Stratocasters and other off-the-shelf models inadequate for their high-octane playing, and were obliged to turn to custom shops and individual craftsmen to obtain "axes" that answered their needs.

By the end of the decade, Eddie Van Halen was using stripped-down, single-pickup guitars with Strat-shaped bodies and powerful vibratos. One source for these hybrids was Charvel Manufacturing – named after Wayne Charvel, who had run a repair and customizing business in Azusa, California, but had sold it in 1978 to his former employee, Grover Jackson. The company's mission to provide musicians with instruments that exactly matched their requirements was enshrined in one of its early catalogs, which stated that "Charvel Mfg. believes very strongly in individual tastes….[there are] absolutely no color or design limitations." However, in 1980, Jackson was approached by another leading Californian rock player, Randy

Rhoads, to build a hot-rodded "Flying V"-style guitar, and was, according to Jackson/Charvel expert Robert Lane, "hesitant to use the Charvel logo on [it] because of its wild shape and contours." The problem was quickly solved: "Grover simply signed his last name on the headstock, and the first Jackson was born!"

Rhoads had recently become lead guitarist for British heavy rocker Ozzy Osbourne, and his high-profile use of the new V-shaped solid led to substantial demand for Grover Jackson's instruments. The following year, Jackson launched a hugely successful new model, the Soloist; it combined a so-called "Superstrat" shape with the neck-through-body design (first seen on Les Paul's "Log" – see pages 38-39) used on the custom Rhoads instruments.

Two Jackson Soloists are featured here, together with a KV1 – the company's most recent take on the V shape.

Opposite page, left and center: *Jackson Soloist SL1, 1998. The Soloist has a recognizably Stratocaster-like shape, although the horns that form the cutaways have been considerably extended. The instrument's neck section, which runs through the center of the body, is maple; the "wings" on either side are poplar. It is fitted with two Seymour Duncan humbucking pickups, and a Floyd Rose vibrato unit that allows dramatic detuning effects.*

Opposite page, far right : *Jackson KV1, 1998. The "King V," Jackson suggests in its publicity, is "a guitar only those with a certain edge to their personality can understand" – and it is endorsed by one of the most powerful players on the current heavy metal scene, Dave Mustaine of Megadeth. It shares the neck-through-body construction **(above, inset)** of the other instruments shown here, and has Seymour Duncan pickups. This model is made from poplar, but the guitar is also available in korina wood.*

Left: *Jackson SLS, 1998. The Soloist Superlite is about 25 percent thinner, and therefore considerably lighter, than the original Soloist. Its body and neck are mahogany, with a slightly contoured flamed maple top and a bound rosewood fingerboard. The pickups are made by Seymour Duncan.*

The characteristic pointed headstock is found on nearly all Jackson guitars.

Jackson's Custom Models

S adly, Randy Rhoads, who commissioned the first Jackson guitar, died in a flying accident while on tour with the Ozzy Osbourne Band in 1982. However, his advocacy of Grover Jackson's instruments encouraged many other hard rock and heavy metal players to adopt them. Among those to do so was his replacement in the Osbourne band, Jake E. Lee, who played Charvel "Strats;" star endorsees for the company's own-name guitars include Phil Collen of Def Leppard and Anthrax's Scott Ian.

The Rhoads guitar remains in Jackson's catalog in a variety of configurations and finishes. In 1995, it received a startling "makeover" when the radically reshaped Roswell Rhoads made its debut. As its name and space age appearance suggest, this instrument was inspired by events in Roswell, New Mexico, where a UFO and its crew of aliens are alleged to have crashed in 1947. Its fingerboard inlays are modeled on another mysterious manifestation – the "crop circles" that sometimes appear in English cornfields. The standard Roswell Rhoads is produced in black or midnight blue, but is also available with custom "interference" finishes, in which the guitar's color seems to change depending on the angle from which it is seen. The special aluminum version illustrated was made in 1996.

Although its founder is no longer directly associated with the firm (he left in 1989), Jackson maintains the tradition of offering an extensive range of choices on made-to-order instruments. The models illustrated here are reworkings of its standard guitars; but the Jackson custom shop can also provide flamboyant graphic finishes, special inlays, and other extras, and offers to build its clients "almost anything they can dream up."

Jacksons have a bold, outrageous quality that makes them ideal and highly sought-after instruments for rock playing. The company acknowledges that its designs are not for everyone, but remains strongly committed to the original and daring approach it has pioneered over the last two decades. As it states in its current catalog, "our goal is not to try and appeal to every last guitar player on earth, but rather to offer the most unique and individually styled instruments in the world."

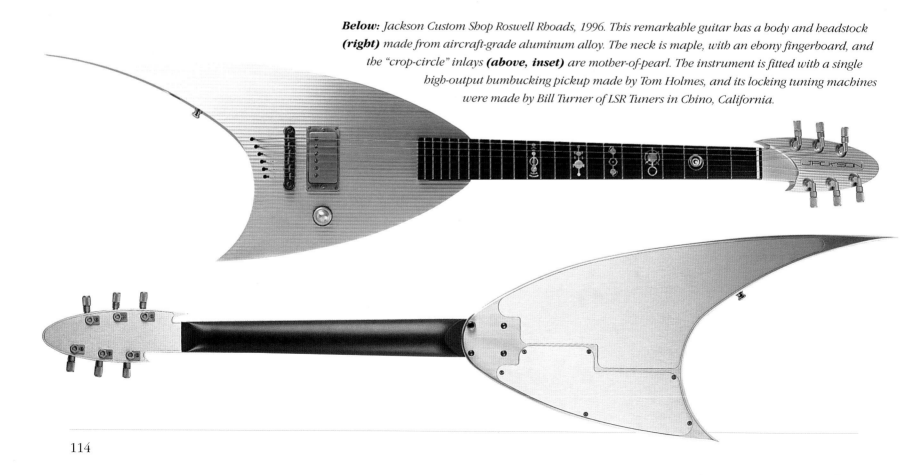

Below: Jackson Custom Shop Roswell Rhoads, 1996. This remarkable guitar has a body and headstock (right) made from aircraft-grade aluminum alloy. The neck is maple, with an ebony fingerboard, and the "crop-circle" inlays (above, inset) are mother-of-pearl. The instrument is fitted with a single high-output humbucking pickup made by Tom Holmes, and its locking tuning machines were made by Bill Turner of LSR Tuners in Chino, California.

Below: *Jackson Custom Shop "Telecaster," 1998. This 1990s version of the Tele would have caused some raised eyebrows at Leo Fender's workshop!*

The Jackson Custom Shop Telecaster has three humbuckers, a Floyd Rose vibrato unit (the "whammy bar," which would be inserted into the socket on the right of the bridge, has been removed for this photograph), and a locking nut to improve tuning stability when using it. Note the reversed headstock, with the tuning machines facing away from the player.

Right and far right: *Jackson Custom Shop "Firebird," 1998. The Gibson Firebird was one of the neck-through-body designs that inspired Grover Jackson at the start of his career. Jackson's own "FB" models take the original concept a few stages further. The example shown here has a reverse-body shape, with the right-hand (treble) horn larger than the bass one, but a standard, non-reversed headstock – unlike its Gibson counterpart. There are two humbucking pickups, and the guitar's tuning machines, like those on the custom Roswell Rhoads, are locking LSRs.*

(ALL INSTRUMENTS ON THESE PAGES COURTESY AKAI/EMI GUITAR DIVISION)

Klein Electric Guitars

Californian luthier Steve Klein's electric guitars look strikingly unconventional, but their appearance is far from being a visual gimmick. These headless instruments are designed to provide optimum balance and ease of playing, and are favored by a long list of famous musicians, including Bill Frisell, Andy Summers, Henry Kaiser, Kenny Wessel (guitarist with Ornette Coleman), and Lou Reed.

Klein, who started making guitars while still in high school in 1967, is based in Sonoma, about 30 miles (50km) north of San Francisco. He is also renowned for his acoustic instruments, and the bodies of his BF-96 and DT-96 electrics are shaped to support the player's right (or striking) arm in the same way that the upper bout of

an acoustic does. Unlike some guitars, they are not neck- or body-heavy, and do not constrict the performer's arm movements by having to be held in position. The design also benefits the left (or fretting) arm, which is given easier access to the higher reaches of the neck by the gently sloping body shape that replaces a conventional cutaway.

Since 1995, the electric division of Steve Klein Guitars has been run by Steve's friend and colleague Lorenzo German, who builds the BF- and DT-96 models (as well as a Klein electric bass) with the assistance of a small staff. However, the third guitar illustrated here, an earlier, custom model known as "The Bird," offers a sharp contrast to the ergonomic perfection of these more recent designs. Described by Lorenzo as "the Anti-Klein guitar," it is heavy, not so comfortable to play – but, as he says, "an amazing art-piece." "The Bird" was commissioned by W.G. "Snuffy" Walden, who had met Steve Klein in Colorado, but left for England with his band, the Stray Dogs, before the instrument was completed. The two men subsequently lost touch; but a few years ago, Steve discovered that Snuffy Walden had returned from overseas and become a leading Los Angeles-based musical director, providing music for major TV shows such as *Roseanne, Thirtysomething* and *The Wonder Years*. Snuffy has now seen the guitar, but has yet to take delivery of it!

Left: Klein BF-96, 1997. The BF- and DT-96 shown here have identical electronics – two Seymour Duncan humbuckers in the neck and bridge positions, and a Seymour Duncan single-coil transducer in the middle (various custom options are also available) but their bodies are made from different woods. The BF-96 is made from swamp ash – a tree that remains immersed in water for several months of the year. The timber used to make the guitars is taken from the lowest, most waterlogged part of the trunk, and the BF-96 is somewhat heavier than its alder or basswood DF- counterpart. It is also produced in a version with hollowed-out cavities inside its body.

(ALL INSTRUMENTS ON
THESE PAGES COURTESY
KLEIN ELECTRIC GUITARS)

Top of page: *Klein DT-96, 1997. Basswood or alder is used on the DT-96; and this basswood
example is fitted with a Novax "Fanned Fret Fingerboard System" (an option on all Klein
electrics). Invented by luthier Ralph Novak, its fret positioning "fans out" from the 12th fret to
provide better overall intonation than is possible with standard horizontal frets.*

Right and inset: *Klein "Bird" custom, early 1970s. This guitar has a highly unusual shape,
although, as Steve Klein comments, "It's patterned after a Les Paul, believe it or not! The critical points
are where your [right] arm rests, and you can see a Les Paul shape in it." The metal decorations are
solid bronze – which adds considerably to the instrument's weight – and its original strap (not shown here)
was made from a camel harness! The modular pickup and bridge units can easily be removed and replaced.*

Rick Turner's "Pretzel" and Model 1 Guitars

Rick Turner, one of America's most creative and respected luthiers, designs and builds his guitars in the Monterey Bay-side city of Santa Cruz. He came to California in 1968, having previously worked as a musician and instrument repairer on the East Coast – where he played guitar in Boston coffee houses, and backed the leading Canadian folk duo Ian and Sylvia. Rick subsequently joined a New York-based rock band, and continued his musical career as a guitarist and bassist after moving west; but by 1969 he had decided that his ambitions lay in electric instrument making.

Rick built his earliest electrics, including the "Pretzel" shown opposite, entirely by hand. Their design was tailored to what could be achieved with a minimum of tooling; as he explains, the Pretzel was "the first instrument where I ran the neck all the way through the body, and added wings onto the side. It was an easy way to attach the neck, and ideally suited to hand building. I think the only electric tool I had at that time was maybe an electric drill."

During this period, Rick became one of a group of highly talented engineers and craftspeople associated with the Grateful Dead. This team eventually coalesced into Alembic, Inc. (see pages 90-91) a company of which he was a co-founder and stockholder. After playing a key role in the design of Alembic's early instruments, he left the company in 1978 to start his own guitar-making business.

Rick's first post-Alembic guitar, the Model 1, caught the attention of Fleetwood Mac's Lindsey Buckingham while it was still on the drawing board. Buckingham ordered one of the new instruments, and Rick delivered an early prototype to him in 1979, during Fleetwod Mac's rehearsals for their *Tusk* tour. He recalls that "after [Lindsey] had been playing the guitar for about two hours, he yelled to his guitar tech, 'You can leave the Strats and the Les Pauls and the Ovations at home – this is all I need!'" Buckingham has used the Model 1 ever since, and it has been featured on many Fleetwood Mac videos and recordings.

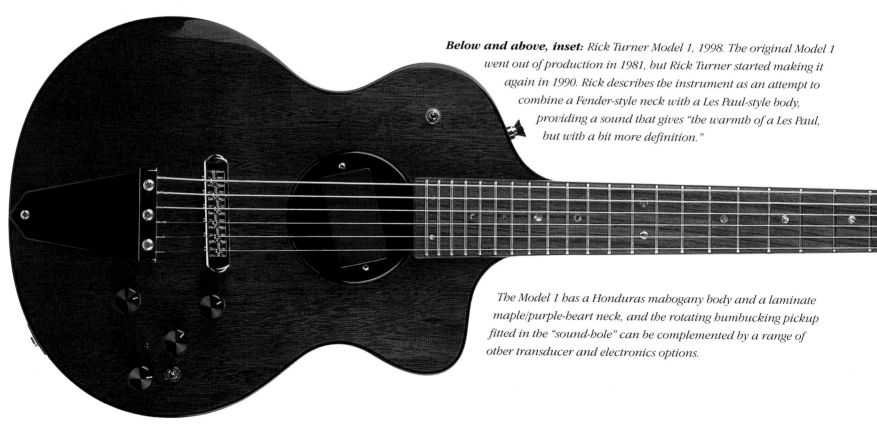

Below and above, inset: Rick Turner Model 1, 1998. The original Model 1 went out of production in 1981, but Rick Turner started making it again in 1990. Rick describes the instrument as an attempt to combine a Fender-style neck with a Les Paul-style body, providing a sound that gives "the warmth of a Les Paul, but with a bit more definition."

The Model 1 has a Honduras mahogany body and a laminate maple/purple-heart neck, and the rotating humbucking pickup fitted in the "sound-hole" can be complemented by a range of other transducer and electronics options.

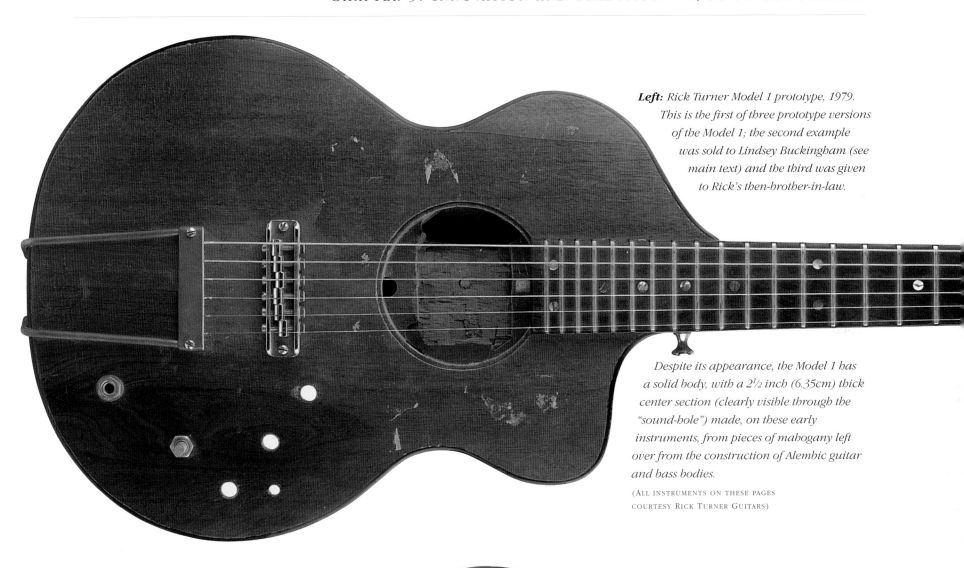

Left: Rick Turner Model 1 prototype, 1979. This is the first of three prototype versions of the Model 1; the second example was sold to Lindsey Buckingham (see main text) and the third was given to Rick's then-brother-in-law.

Despite its appearance, the Model 1 has a solid body, with a 2½ inch (6.35cm) thick center section (clearly visible through the "sound-hole") made, on these early instruments, from pieces of mahogany left over from the construction of Alembic guitar and bass bodies.

(ALL INSTRUMENTS ON THESE PAGES COURTESY RICK TURNER GUITARS)

Lower right: *Rick Turner "Pretzel," 1969. This hand-made guitar, with the carved-out body shape that gives it its nickname, shares some of the characteristics of early Alembic instruments (see pages 90-91).*

Like the Alembics, the "Pretzel" has a neck-through-body construction – an alternative to gluing in or bolting on the neck, first used by Rickenbacker in the 1950s before being taken up by Gibson and a number of other manufacturers.

Rick Turner's Renaissance and Model T Guitars

As a luthier, Rick Turner is especially interested in what he calls "the big fuzzy grey area between pure acoustic and pure electric. That's where most of what I do is done." Good "acoustic" sound is notoriously hard to obtain from amplified instruments (especially in noisy, unpredictable onstage settings), and even the finest acoustic guitars will give disappointing results when used with unsuitable added-on pickups. Rick's researches have convinced him of the need for an acoustic/electric that can provide what he calls an "optimum platform" for its pickup,

and his "Renaissance" models are conceived as fully integrated systems – with instrument, transducer, and electronics all designed to operate together effectively.

The Renaissance has many electric-style features, including a solid, Gibson 335-type center body section with hollow cavities on either side, a bolt-on neck, a slim, fast-playing fingerboard, and a deep cutaway. But other aspects of its construction – the braced, solid wood top, the overall shape and light weight – are typical of an acoustic instrument. Rick Turner recognizes the guitar's "hybrid" status by designating it

Below: Rick Turner Model T, 1998. The Model T has a Formica-laminate top and back (in a pattern Formica have named "Rosetta Boomerang"), and a Honduras mahogany body core.

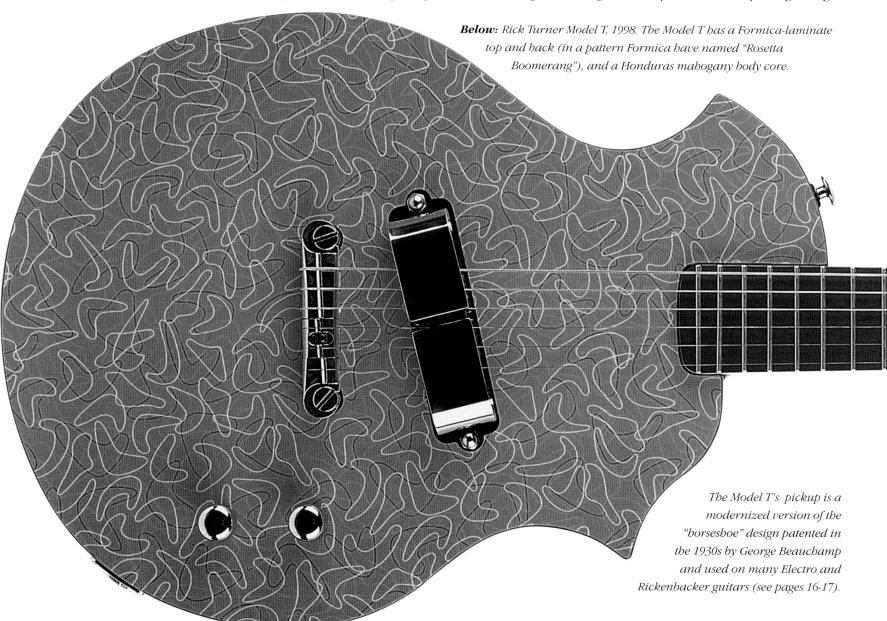

The Model T's pickup is a modernized version of the "horseshoe" design patented in the 1930s by George Beauchamp and used on many Electro and Rickenbacker guitars (see pages 16-17).

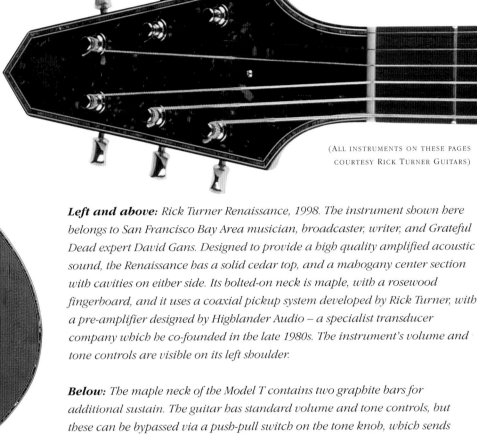

(ALL INSTRUMENTS ON THESE PAGES
COURTESY RICK TURNER GUITARS)

Left and above: Rick Turner Renaissance, 1998. *The instrument shown here belongs to San Francisco Bay Area musician, broadcaster, writer, and Grateful Dead expert David Gans. Designed to provide a high quality amplified acoustic sound, the Renaissance has a solid cedar top, and a mahogany center section with cavities on either side. Its bolted-on neck is maple, with a rosewood fingerboard, and it uses a coaxial pickup system developed by Rick Turner, with a pre-amplifier designed by Highlander Audio – a specialist transducer company which he co-founded in the late 1980s. The instrument's volume and tone controls are visible on its left shoulder.*

Below: The maple neck of the Model T contains two graphite bars for additional sustain. The guitar has standard volume and tone controls, but these can be bypassed via a push-pull switch on the tone knob, which sends the pickup output direct to the amplifier.

an "ampli-coustic," and he produces it in different configurations – there are standard six-string, twelve-string, baritone, and nylon-strung versions.

Rick Turner has a refreshingly straightforward attitude to the complex process of creating a new instrument. He describes it as "being like a slot machine – but instead of three or four windows there may be twenty or thirty, and each one of those represents something important in the design. And what happens is that ideas pile up in the wheels behind the windows, and every now and then I can pull the lever, and the windows will all come up cherries – and I've got a new guitar design!" Rick certainly hit the jackpot with his Model T (shown opposite), which won the "Best of Show" prize for "retro" guitars at the 1996 NAMM (National Association of Music Merchants) show. Its appearance was inspired by the oddly-shaped range of guitars and mandolins manufactured by the Chicago-based Kay company from the late 1920s until the mid-1930s, although these did not have the Model T's Formica covering. Rick says the instrument epitomizes "taste carried to its absolute extreme!"

121

Jerry Jones Guitars

Nashville-based luthier Jerry Jones is dedicated to recreating the classic Danelectro, Silvertone, and Coral electric guitar designs of Nathan Daniel (see pages 50-51). Jerry, who was born in Jackson, Mississippi, has been making guitars in Music City since the early 1980s. He started out by producing a line of self-designed custom models, but a visit from a customer with a damaged Silvertone soon led to a change in direction. Jerry had always been interested in Nathan Daniel's instruments, and as he explains, "This was the first time I ever really got to have one in my shop for repairs. I sat down and thought, 'This is more like the kind of guitar that I would build for myself – rather than one of the custom guitars I was building for other people.' So I [decided] I'd just make myself one." Jerry started work on his prototype instrument (shown opposite) in 1984, but put it aside when another client commissioned a Danelectro-style Longhorn six-string bass from him – an event which, in Jerry's words, "opened up the opportunity to make a whole line of [Daniel-inspired] guitars." The prototype remains un-finished, but is still used regularly for testing pick-ups.

Like Nathan Daniel, Jerry builds his guitar tops and backs from Masonite, and covers their sides with vinyl. However, he has replaced their V-shaped truss rods with a more modern, adjustable design, and now makes their necks out of maple, not poplar. He also uses high-technology CNC (computer numeric control) systems to carve out bodies and necks – this speeds up production, enabling him and his four employees to complete 16 guitars a week.

Jerry relishes the simplicity and unpretentiousness of Nathan Daniel's instruments, and remembers their creator with admiration. In 1991, he visited Daniel in Hawaii, and recalls the fascination of "being able to sit down and talk to him about all this stuff – it was just incredible." He is uncertain about the origins of the Danelectro's distinctive shape, but comments that "if that design had been drawn out on a napkin in some diner back in the 1950s, I'd love to have that napkin!"

Right: Jerry Jones N1 G3, 1998. A single-cutaway guitar fitted with three "lipstick-tube" pickups (Jerry also makes twelve-string and baritone models with the same body shape). The top and back are Masonite (hardboard), and the internal center and bridge blocks are poplar. The headstocks on Jerry Jones guitars retain the classic "Coke-bottle" shape of the Danelectro originals. Such instruments are available in a variety of standard and custom colors.

Left and opposite page, top left: Jerry Jones Longhorn six-string bass, 1998. In 1956, Nathan Daniel was the first guitar maker to produce a six-string bass; he introduced the double-cutaway "Longhorn" shape seen here in 1958, using it for six- and four-string basses. Jerry produces his own versions of these models, as well as the "guitarlin" (a standard six-string with the Longhorn shape); he has also developed a Longhorn doubleneck, combining six-string guitar and six-string bass.

Construction of the prototype *(right)* closely follows Nathan Daniel's original design; a solid block of wood runs down the center of the body to the bridge, which is supported by another block (the two pieces of wood combine in an inverted "T" shape), and the guitar's two side sections are hollow.

(ALL INSTRUMENTS ON THESE PAGES COURTESY JERRY JONES GUITARS)

Below: *Jerry Jones prototype, 1984. This unfinished instrument was Jerry's first attempt at a Danelectro-style guitar.*

Above left: *Jerry Jones Shorthorn, 1998. A more conventional double-cutaway design, available in two- or three-pickup versions. The attractively shaped white pickguard of the Shorthorn closely resembles the ones fitted to Nathan Daniel's Silvertone guitars (manufactured for the Sears company in the 1950s and 1960s). As Jerry Jones' catalog puts it, "They don't make 'em like they used to – so we do!"*

Guitars by Hugh Manson

The southwest of England's peaceful rural environment has attracted a number of leading British luthiers. One of the most distinguished of these, Hugh Manson, has lived and worked in the village of Sandford, near Exeter, for the last 12 years. He makes a wide variety of guitars, from the "Classic" range of Tele- and Strat-style six-strings (sold at his music stores in Exeter and Plymouth) to custom models for famous players such as Martin Barre from Jethro Tull and Led Zeppelin's John Paul Jones.

Hugh built his first guitar at the age of 14, and has been a professional luthier for the last two decades. His success did not come overnight: as he explains, "First you have to get a foot in the door, and until you get a name it's very difficult." One guitar design that helped to establish his reputation, the Kestrel electric, originally sold for under £300, but currently fetches well over double that amount on the second-hand market. Hugh now produces about 35 handmade instruments a year, with a delivery time of 12 to 15 weeks, and has a preference for more unusual commissions; his output includes "mandolas, mandolins – everything with frets or without frets on. I made Cliff Richard's electric sitar, and I've made three-necks, four-necks, things with lights on, things with smoke coming out of them….That's really what I do, and what I want to do. I don't like to make the same guitar day in, day out."

One of the advantages of Hugh Manson's rural location is its proximity to high quality, sustainable sources of timber, and he chooses and matches the woods for his instruments with as much care as any acoustic luthier, commenting that "the art of making electric guitars is tailoring the wood to the sound." The three instruments seen here – a standard solid-body, a hollow-chambered jazz archtop, and a highly unusual eight-string model – display very different approaches to this crucial task, but share the striking visual appearance and superior playability that are hallmarks of all Manson electrics. Some of Hugh's more exotic guitars, including a double- and a triple-neck, are featured on pages 144-145.

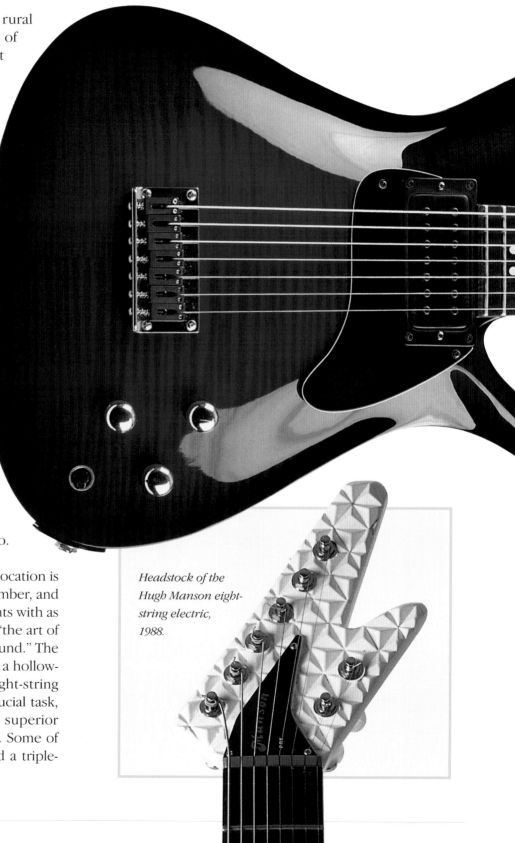

Headstock of the Hugh Manson eight-string electric, 1988.

Below left: *Hugh Manson Classic S, 1998. While its overall body shape is familiar, the "S" offers a number of special features, including Seymour Duncan pickups – a humbucker and two single-coils – and a vibrato unit designed by Trevor Wilkinson (currently working with Patrick Eggle Guitars in Birmingham, see pages 126-129). The front of the Classic S is Canadian quilted maple, and its back and sides are swamp ash. Bird's-eye maple is used for the neck, which has a rosewood fingerboard.* (COURTESY HUGH MANSON)

Above left: *Hugh Manson seven-string archtop guitar, 1998. This "neck-through-body" guitar was designed for a jazz player, who wanted a richer, more "hollow" sound than a typical rock instrument provides. Hugh Manson achieved it by building several air chambers between its flamed maple front and poplar sides. The five-piece neck is made from maple and American black walnut, with an ebony fingerboard. There is a Christian piezo-electric transducer (with a pre-amp designed by Hugh) built into the bridge saddles, providing a more "acoustic" sound that can be combined with the output from the Kent Armstrong humbucking pickup via a "pan" control on the body. The extra bass string extends the instrument's compass by a fifth.* (COURTESY HUGH MANSON)

Right and opposite page, bottom: *Hugh Manson eight-string electric, 1988. The guitar's added top and bottom strings are both tuned to A (three octaves apart), and the triangular decorations on its body were all carved by hand.*

(COURTESY PAUL EVANS)

*The neck of the eight-string electric (**above**) features inset LEDs (light-emitting diodes), connected to a power supply via a network of wires that run through tiny holes drilled through the body.*

Patrick Eggle Guitars

*I*n 1990, a young guitar maker from the English Midlands, Patrick Eggle, was displaying his wares at a local trade fair. He had only a small number of instruments on show, but one of the visitors to his booth, Andrew Selby, was so impressed with their quality and originality that he decided to set up a company to manufacture them. Just a year later, the new firm, Patrick Eggle Guitars, launched a production version of the model Selby had seen at the fair. This instrument, the Berlin, quickly established itself as a modern classic, and it is currently used by a string of major players, including Tony Iommi of Black Sabbath, Big Country's Bruce Watson, Bill Nelson, Midge Ure, and Ali and Robin Campbell of UB40.

By the mid-1990s, the company was producing up to 2,000 electrics, acoustics, and basses a year; but more recently, it has undergone a fundamental reorganization, moving from its original home in Coventry to smaller, newly converted premises in Birmingham. It has also rationalized its range of models, and now makes only electric guitars – various versions of the Berlin, as well as the Anniversary, Legend, Vintage Classic, and the new Fret King range (shown on pages 128-129). These are built using tools and equipment taken from the firm's old Coventry plant – including a neck profiler

converted from a machine for making rifle butts!

Sales Director Peter Goalby welcomes the changes, while acknowledging that Patrick Eggle Guitars has had to face "a lot of tears and a lot of heartache" to reach its present, impressive level of success. The company now employs a much smaller staff than the 30-strong workforce once based in Coventry, currently produces about 20 to 25 instruments a month, and is recognized as one of the UK's most successful guitar manufacturers.

Patrick Eggle himself left the business in 1994, although he remains on excellent terms with his former colleagues, and has visited the new factory in Birmingham. Peter Goalby explains that "Pat never wanted to be involved in a manufacturing situation. He's a designer, and he designed what became a world-class guitar – and you don't do that every day".

Opposite page, main picture: *Patrick Eggle Custom Berlin Pro, 1998. The Berlin is available in a variety of configurations, and with a 22- or 24-fret fingerboard. The instrument has a maple top (finished in "Adriatic Burst") and a mahogany body; its hardware (including the distinctive Spertzel Trimlok locking tuning machines seen **below, left and right**) is finished in gold, and its "falling maple leaf" fingerboard inlays **(above, inset)** are abalone*

Below: *The Patrick Eggle Custom Berlin Pro is fitted with two Seymour Duncan humbuckers (an Alnico Pro II in the neck and a Custom Custom at the bridge) and has a Fishman VS50 piezo system built into its bridge/vibrato unit. This provides an acoustic-type tone that can be mixed in with the other pickups.*

Above right: *Patrick Eggle Berlin Legend, 1998. This model is based on a Limited Edition guitar endorsed by Big Jim Sullivan – a famous British session player who for many years was the guitarist in Tom Jones' backing band. It has a lightweight swamp ash body with a highly figured maple top, a maple neck, and an ebony fingerboard. The pickups are Seymour Duncan "Live" humbuckers, and the vibrato unit (as on the Custom Berlin Pro) is a VS100 unit designed by Patrick Eggle Guitars' Creative Director, Trevor Wilkinson (see pages 128-129).*

Top of page: *Patrick Eggle Berlin Pro HT, 1998. The Pro HT is the fixed-bridge, non-vibrato version of the Berlin. It features the same electronics as the Custom model, but without the Fishman pickup. The Berlin's circuitry is designed for maximum versatility and convenience. Its upper knob is a volume control, while the lower knob is a three-position rotary switch, allowing the pickups to be used in single-coil or humbucking modes, or as humbuckers via a special electronic filter providing a rich, bluesy sound.*

(ALL INSTRUMENTS ON THESE PAGES COURTESY PATRICK EGGLE GUITARS)

Eggle's "Fret King" Esprit Range

*P*atrick Eggle Guitars' most recent additions to its range are the "Fret King" Esprit models, a trio of strikingly shaped solid-bodies launched in late 1998. They were designed by the company's Creative Director, Trevor Wilkinson – an influential name in the electric guitar world, famous for the widely used vibrato unit that bears his name. He explains that the Esprits, his first project for Eggle, are aimed at "people who are wanting something a little different from a Strat," and there is certainly nothing run-of-the-mill about these distinctive and reasonably priced new instruments.

The Esprits' shape suggests a cross between a Fender Jazzmaster and a Gibson Firebird, or perhaps one of the Gibson "modernistic" guitars developed in the late 1950s (see pages 84-85). All three models have reversed headstocks, with six-in-line tuning machines facing away from the player, but non-reverse bodies. Like the original "modernistics" (the Explorer and the Flying V) the Esprits are made from korina (sometimes known as limba) wood – a mahogany-like African timber first used for lutherie by Gibson in the early 1950s.

The new range offers a variety of pickup configurations. The Fret King Esprit 1 (not illustrated here) and Esprit 3 are fitted with Gotoh-made replicas of the classic Gibson single-coil P-90 "soapbar" pickup. (This vintage transducer, originally fitted to a wide range of classic Gibson guitars, from the ES-5 and ES-175 to the Les Paul and the Firebird, is as popular as ever; another version of it can be seen on the Paul Reed Smith "McCarty Soapbar" model featured on pages 142-143.) By contrast, the top-of-the-range Esprit 5 has two humbucking pickups, wired to a three-way coil-tapping switch in the same way as Patrick Eggle's Berlin models. This arrangement allows a wide range of tonal variation, including useful approximations of Strat-type single-coil sounds.

The three Fret King Esprits are an ingenious combination of "retro" features and contemporary design, and were awarded the "Best Guitar of the Show" accolade when they were displayed at the 1998 Frankfurt Music Fair. The Fret King range will soon be augmented by two new models designed by Trevor Wilkinson, the Corona and the Country Squire.

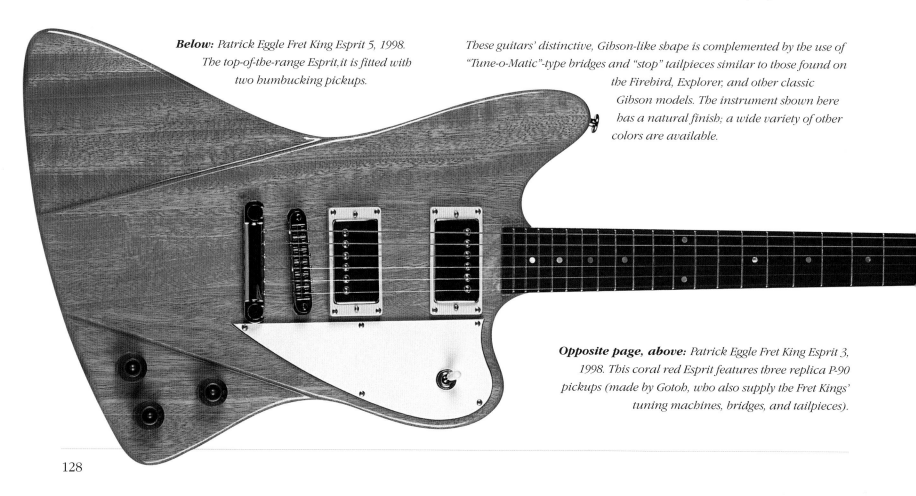

Below: *Patrick Eggle Fret King Esprit 5, 1998. The top-of-the-range Esprit, it is fitted with two humbucking pickups.*

These guitars' distinctive, Gibson-like shape is complemented by the use of "Tune-o-Matic"-type bridges and "stop" tailpieces similar to those found on the Firebird, Explorer, and other classic Gibson models. The instrument shown here has a natural finish; a wide variety of other colors are available.

Opposite page, above: *Patrick Eggle Fret King Esprit 3, 1998. This coral red Esprit features three replica P-90 pickups (made by Gotoh, who also supply the Fret Kings' tuning machines, bridges, and tailpieces).*

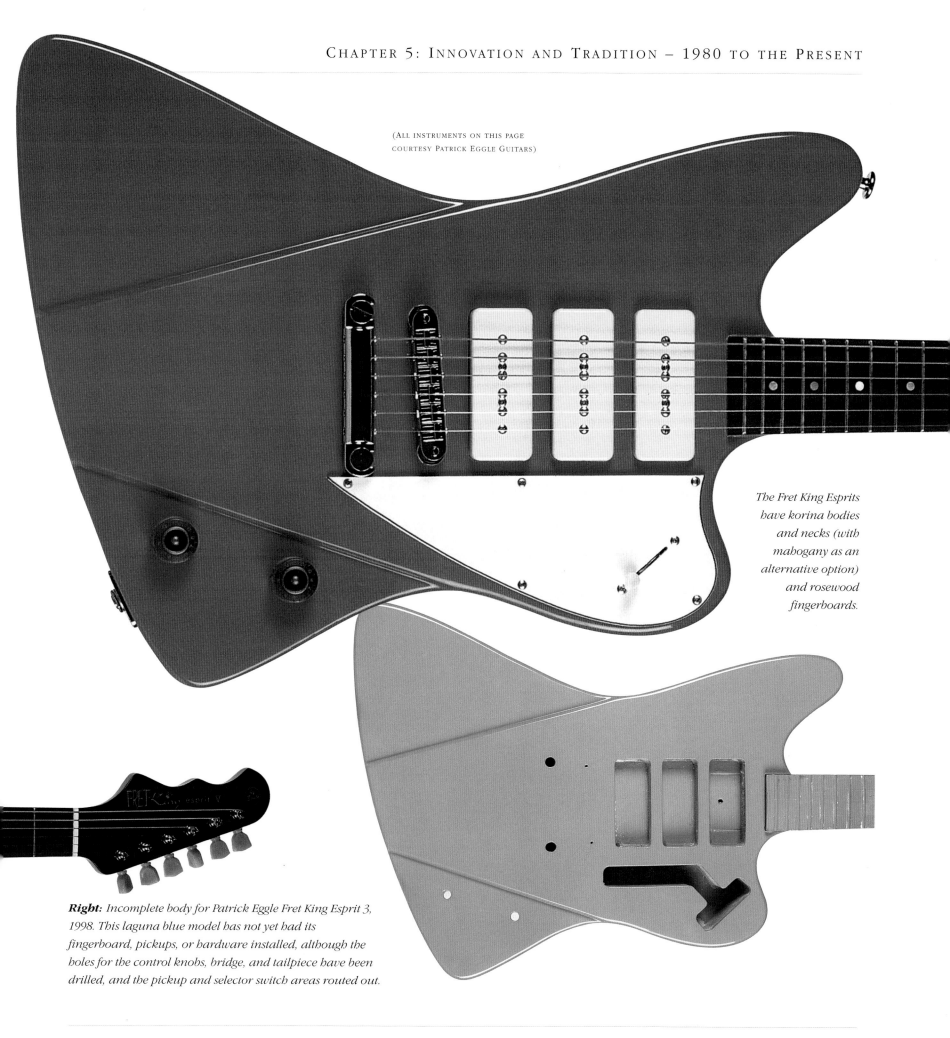

(ALL INSTRUMENTS ON THIS PAGE
COURTESY PATRICK EGGLE GUITARS)

*The Fret King Esprits
have korina bodies
and necks (with
mahogany as an
alternative option)
and rosewood
fingerboards.*

Right: *Incomplete body for Patrick Eggle Fret King Esprit 3,
1998. This laguna blue model has not yet had its
fingerboard, pickups, or hardware installed, although the
holes for the control knobs, bridge, and tailpiece have been
drilled, and the pickup and selector switch areas routed out.*

Electric Guitars by Robert Benedetto

Robert Benedetto, of East Stroudsburg, Pennsylvania, is recognized as today's finest archtop luthier. In the last 30 years, he has designed instruments for many leading players, from Johnny Smith and Chuck Wayne to Andy Summers and Earl Klugh, and a recent commission from the great American jazz guitarist Kenny Burrell (b.1931) has given him particular pleasure. As Bob explains, "In 1966, I bought my very first jazz guitar album, [Kenny Burrell's] *Man at Work*. He instantly became a great inspiration, [and] I felt strongly that someday I would make him a guitar. Imagine my excitement when I received a phone call from Kenny 30 years later: 'Bob, I'd like to talk with you about making me a guitar'. Wow, I'm living my dream!"

The original plan was for Benedetto to build a single, custom instrument for Burrell, but it was subsequently decided to produce a limited edition "Kenny Burrell" model, incorporating a number of special features developed by its two creators. The guitar has a tapered body depth (widening from neck to tailpiece) which, in Kenny Burrell's words, makes

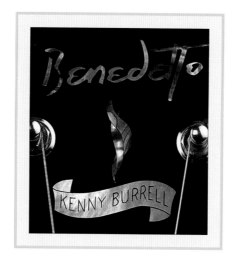

it "the most comfortable [instrument] you'll ever play," and is fitted with a single Benedetto B-6 pickup. Kenny first used the prototype in public at The Chinery Collection and Smithsonian Institution's "Blue Guitar" concert in June 1998. His response to Bob Benedetto's craftsmanship is simple and heartfelt: "You made my dreams come true."

Benedetto is the most prolific independent maker of seven-string archtops, and the example shown here was custom-built for one of the instrument's finest exponents, jazz guitarist Jimmy Bruno. It has a Benedetto B-7 humbucking pickup fitted directly onto its top, but retains an excellent acoustic sound; its volume and tone controls are positioned near the edge of the top to prevent them interfering with vibrations from the bridge.

On "Il Colibri" Bob has again been at pains to maximize the guitar's acoustic tone, using an arched construction for the top and back, and leaving openings around the two pickups for the sound to escape. This beautiful instrument, made for guitarist Carl Trollinger, also features fine mother-of-pearl and abalone inlays on its headstock, fingerboard, and tailpiece.

Left: Benedetto custom "Kenny Burrell" model (prototype), 1998. This 17-inch (43.2cm) model (16-inch and 18-inch sizes are also available) has a top of select European spruce, a back and sides of select, highly flamed European maple, and a three-piece neck of flamed American maple.

Its tapered body is 2 5/8 inches (6.7cm) deep at the neck, gently broadening to 3 7/16 inches (8.7cm) at the tailpiece. The inlay motifs are abalone, and Kenny Burrell's name is engraved in a mother-of-pearl ribbon on the headstock.

(COURTESY ROBERT BENEDETTO; PHOTOGRAPH BY JOHN BENDER)

Right and bottom right: Benedetto "Il Colibri," 1995. The body and neck are made from American bird's-eye maple (grown in the northeastern U.S.A.) and the ebony tailpiece is veneered with exotic wood burl, which is also used for the pickguard and headstock. The instrument has an ebony fingerboard, two humbucking pickups, and Schaller machine heads with mother-of-pearl buttons.

(Courtesy Carl Trollinger)

Right: Benedetto seven-string, custom-built for Jimmy Bruno, 1995. All the woods used on this 16-inch guitar are American: its top is Sitka spruce, its back and sides flamed Big Leaf maple, and its fittings ebony. The "Jimmy Bruno" inlay on the tailpiece is mother-of-pearl. The finish is Benedetto's signature honey blonde color. The instrument's medium-high string action (preferred by Bruno) contributes to its powerful acoustic and electric sound.

(Courtesy Jimmy Bruno)

Rosendean Guitars

Having a guitar custom-made is not dissimilar to being measured for a Savile Row suit. Every contour of the instrument, and every aspect of its look and feel, can be precisely tailored to a player's needs, with results that combine comfort and elegance with the highest quality and durability. Trevor Dean, whose one-man company, Rosendean, is based in the southern English town of Woking, has been building custom guitars professionally since 1989. His best-known client is the distinguished British jazzman John Etheridge, who commissioned the six-string Black Ruby model seen below. Etheridge is a hard-working player with a vigorous playing style, and the Black Ruby is designed to withstand a good deal of wear and tear. Its back and sides are made from black-eyed Persian larch, giving exceptional lightness and strength, and Trevor has protected the edges of the body with plastic binding. The instrument also offers an impressive range of tones, and its six-way control circuit and special high-pass filters ensure that, in Trevor's own words, there is always "treble to burn."

The seven-string version of the Black Ruby bears a family resemblance to the Etheridge model, but has a mahogany back and sides, wooden bindings, and a single neck pickup. Its owner asked for a brass tailpiece covered in wood; Trevor normally uses nickel tailpieces like the one on the third Rosendean model shown here, a Black Diamond archtop made for musician Stewart Cockett. In a recent article published in *Jazz Guitar International,* Stewart recalls how, while the instrument was being built, he would call at Trevor's workshop every week to check on its development. "From November 1997 the guitar progressed quickly…Eventually the neck was fitted and I could sit [it] on my knee and get a sense of its size and balance. I was impatient to hear it, but weeks of finishing and polishing were still to come before strings went on and we heard how it would sound." The completed guitar proved to be well worth the wait. Stewart describes it as "quite fantastic," and characterizes its tone as "full, smooth, evenly balanced and totally inspiring…[it] will stimulate a whole new musical direction for me."

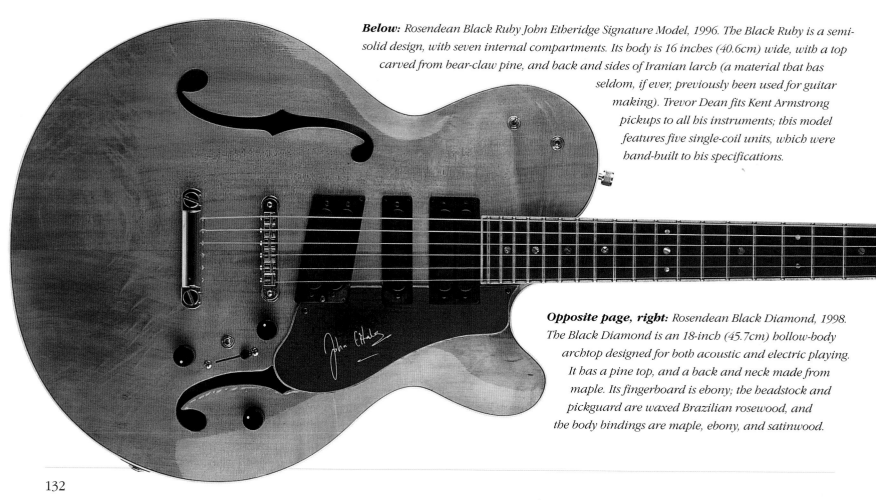

Below: *Rosendean Black Ruby John Etheridge Signature Model, 1996. The Black Ruby is a semi-solid design, with seven internal compartments. Its body is 16 inches (40.6cm) wide, with a top carved from bear-claw pine, and back and sides of Iranian larch (a material that has seldom, if ever, previously been used for guitar making). Trevor Dean fits Kent Armstrong pickups to all his instruments; this model features five single-coil units, which were hand-built to his specifications.*

Opposite page, right: *Rosendean Black Diamond, 1998. The Black Diamond is an 18-inch (45.7cm) hollow-body archtop designed for both acoustic and electric playing. It has a pine top, and a back and neck made from maple. Its fingerboard is ebony; the headstock and pickguard are waxed Brazilian rosewood, and the body bindings are maple, ebony, and satinwood.*

Both left : *Rosendean Black Ruby seven-string, c.1995. A 16-inch (40.6cm) guitar (like its six-string counterpart), this instrument has a pine top and mahogany back and sides. Its pickup is a Kent Armstrong humbucker, with volume and tone controls mounted unobtrusively on the pickguard. The distinctive single-cutaway body shape on Trevor Dean's guitars is derived from the designs of Emile Grimshaw (1880–1943), a distinguished British luthier who was also famous for his banjos.*

(ALL INSTRUMENTS ON THESE PAGES COURTESY TREVOR DEAN)

The Rosendean Black Diamond's natural blonde finish, nickel-plated hardware, and abalone dot markers all contribute to its simple, but elegant appearance; its owner, Stewart Cockett, wanted it to look more like a 40-year-old vintage model than an obviously new guitar.

Mark Knopfler's Pensa Guitars

Custom-designed guitars by Rudy Pensa are played by an impressive list of world-famous performers, including Mark Knopfler, Eric Clapton, and Lou Reed. His instruments, created in the workshop of his music store on West 48th Street in Manhattan (his base since the 1980s), originally carried the Pensa-Suhr label, and it was John Suhr, described as Rudy's "repair guru," who was responsible for building the model that first brought the two men international attention. This guitar – Pensa-Suhr No. 001 – was commissioned by Mark Knopfler, and its design evolved from a drawing made on a napkin while he and Rudy were having lunch! The finished instrument (illustrated here) debuted in 1988 during Dire Straits' appearance at Nelson Mandela's 70th birthday concert (broadcast live throughout the world at a time when the future President of South Africa was still in prison) and Mark Knopfler has gone on to use it for many other major performances and recordings. It features EMG pickups, a Floyd-Rose bridge, and a beautiful one-piece top made from quilted maple. Mark, who possesses a wide range

of vintage electrics, confirms that the Pensa-Suhr is something special: "[It] enables me to play with a lot more power than a Strat, and it's more flexible. I've got more range on it than most other guitars." He also owns several other Pensa-Suhrs, including a synthesizer-guitar built to control his Synclavier system, and a black model, dating from 1987, and fitted – like Pensa-Suhr No. 001 – with EMG pickups.

In 1990, John Suhr and Rudy Pensa parted company; Suhr spent the next few years working for Fender's Custom Shop, and has recently started his own lutherie business. Meanwhile, Rudy Pensa has continued to design superb electric instrument for Mark Knopfler and other distinguished customers. In 1993, Knopfler took delivery of a new Pensa solid-body which has a flamed koa top and three single-coil pickups made by Lindy Fralin, a pickup designer and manufacturer who specializes in creating vintage-sounding transducers for Telecaster- and Strat-type guitars. Mark's most recent Pensa, dating from 1996, also uses Fralin pickups, but this model features active circuitry, as well as a shorter, Gibson-style scale length.

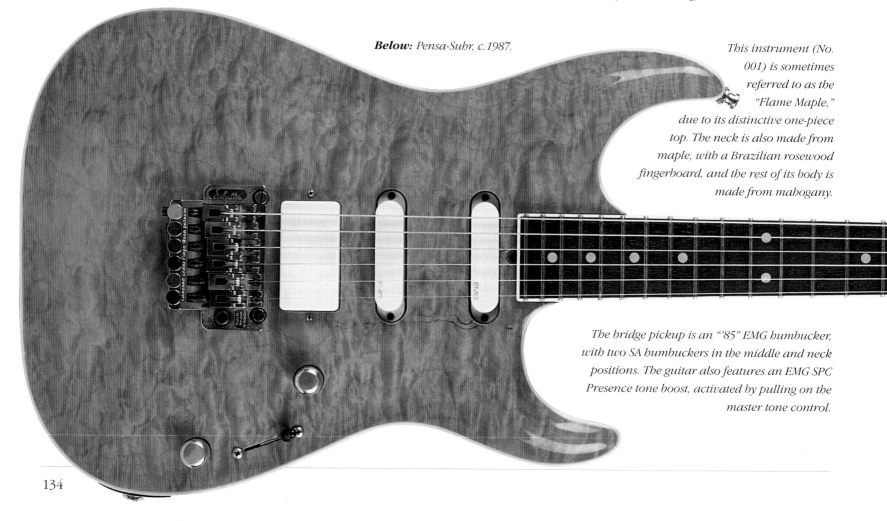

Below: Pensa-Suhr, c.1987.

This instrument (No. 001) is sometimes referred to as the "Flame Maple," due to its distinctive one-piece top. The neck is also made from maple, with a Brazilian rosewood fingerboard, and the rest of its body is made from mahogany.

The bridge pickup is an "'85" EMG humbucker, with two SA humbuckers in the middle and neck positions. The guitar also features an EMG SPC Presence tone boost, activated by pulling on the master tone control.

__Below:__ Pensa Custom, 1996. Another of Mark Knopfler's Pensas, also sporting a flamed maple top and mahogany back. The pickups are by Lindy Fralin (with active electronics) and, unlike the other instruments shown here, the guitar is fitted with a "stop" tailpiece.

(ALL INSTRUMENTS ON THESE PAGES COURTESY MARK KNOPFLER)

__Above, top left:__ Pensa Custom, c. 1993. The Lindy Fralin-designed pickups on this model, also made for Mark Knopfler, are "'54s," designed to recreate the sound of an early Fender Stratocaster (the Strat was first introduced in 1954). The instrument has a flamed koa top, and a mahogany back.

__Right:__ The headstock of the Pensa-Suhr (seen from the back).

Hybrids and Curiosities

The earliest electric guitars were conceived as working tools rather than props or art objects, but performers quickly recognized the instrument's visual and theatrical possibilities. Onstage, it could be posed with as well as played, used suggestively or aggressively, and even smashed up to excite an audience. It was also comparatively simple to make solid-bodied electrics in unusual shapes and finishes. One of the first artists to feature such instruments was rhythm and blues star Bo Diddley (b.1928), who commissioned the Gretsch company to build him several guitars with oblong bodies, and at least one covered in fur! Billy Gibbons and Dusty Hill of ZZ Top followed in Diddley's footsteps with their automobile- and Texas-shaped instruments, and a number of heavy metal guitarists favor even more outlandish custom designs.

However, the "Betty Boop" guitar shown here takes the concept of decorative bodywork several stages further. It was made in about 1984 by Johnson of Los Angeles for Earl Slick, best known as the guitarist on David Bowie's *Young Americans* and *Station To Station*. Betty herself probably has rather different tastes in music – her cartoon films, originally made by animator Max Fleischer, sometimes featured guests like Louis Armstrong, Cab Calloway, and Rudy Vallee – but she seems to

have survived her transformation from celluloid into wood and steel remarkably well. Other Johnson creations include guitars shaped like spaceships and machine-guns.

The Fisher "Saturn V," with a rocket-style body that owes its inspiration to NASA, was commissioned by Memphis-based blues guitarist Eric Gales. Eric signed his first recording contract at the age of only 15, winning the "Best New Talent" category in *Guitar World* magazine's Readers' Poll only a year later. He has subsequently made a number of highly acclaimed albums, and his two brothers, Eugene and Manuel, are also talented players.

The third instrument on these pages is a Gibson guitar harp dating from 1993. It was designed by Roger Giffin, an English luthier who was in charge of Gibson's Los Angeles-based Custom Shop for five years, and later worked for its Research and Development department. Giffin now runs his own successful lutherie business in California's San Fernando Valley.

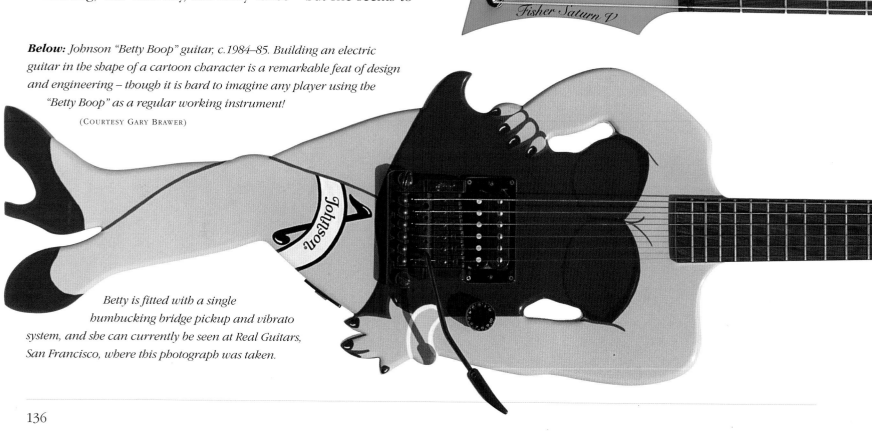

Below: *Johnson "Betty Boop" guitar, c.1984–85. Building an electric guitar in the shape of a cartoon character is a remarkable feat of design and engineering – though it is hard to imagine any player using the "Betty Boop" as a regular working instrument!*

(COURTESY GARY BRAWER)

Betty is fitted with a single humbucking bridge pickup and vibrato system, and she can currently be seen at Real Guitars, San Francisco, where this photograph was taken.

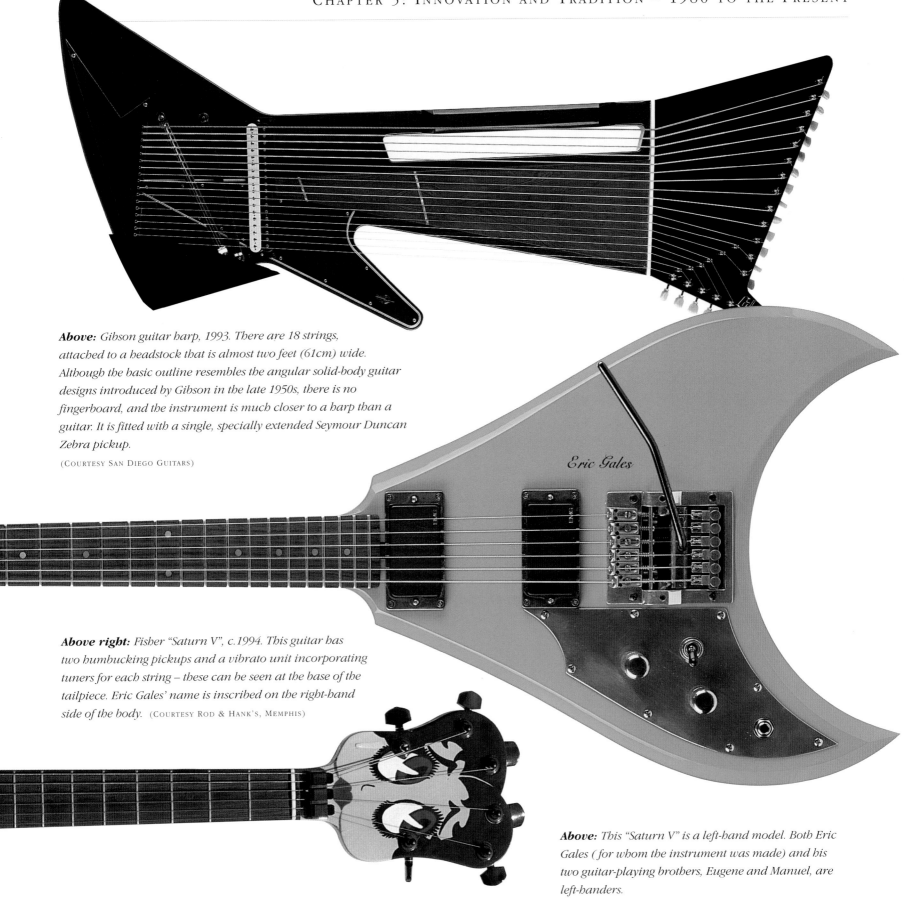

Above: *Gibson guitar harp, 1993. There are 18 strings, attached to a headstock that is almost two feet (61cm) wide. Although the basic outline resembles the angular solid-body guitar designs introduced by Gibson in the late 1950s, there is no fingerboard, and the instrument is much closer to a harp than a guitar. It is fitted with a single, specially extended Seymour Duncan Zebra pickup.*

(COURTESY SAN DIEGO GUITARS)

Above right: *Fisher "Saturn V", c.1994. This guitar has two humbucking pickups and a vibrato unit incorporating tuners for each string – these can be seen at the base of the tailpiece. Eric Gales' name is inscribed on the right-hand side of the body.* (COURTESY ROD & HANK'S, MEMPHIS)

Above: *This "Saturn V" is a left-hand model. Both Eric Gales (for whom the instrument was made) and his two guitar-playing brothers, Eugene and Manuel, are left-handers.*

SECTION FOUR:
Today and Tomorrow

Like its acoustic counterpart, the electric guitar has suffered occasional periods of reduced popularity, but its survival has never been seriously threatened. Even synthesizers and samplers have failed to supplant it; in fact, a number of manufacturers now produce MIDI controllers that permit signals derived from guitar strings to trigger synth modules, with varying degrees of success. Other electronic innovations have proved more popular with players – like the piezo-electric pickup systems fitted to the Patrick Eggle Custom Pro (pages 126-127) and the Parker Fly (pages 142-143), which offer a useful approximation of acoustic guitar tone that can be combined with the instrument's "regular" sound. The use of stereo for guitars is also gradually growing, although the need for a pair of amplifiers and speakers onstage still deters some musicians (and their roadies!).

Stereo circuitry comes into its own on Emmett Chapman's Stick (see pages 146-147), the pickup of which allows bass and melody strings to be routed to individual audio channels on a mixing desk, where they can be processed separately before being panned into place. Such sonic flexibility is only one small aspect of Chapman's remarkably versatile design; and today, more than 25 years since the Stick's introduction, there seems little doubt that this distinctive new member of the electric guitar family is here to stay.

Alongside such innovative recent instruments, the final chapter in this book includes other unashamedly "retro" models paying respectful homage to the great designs of the past and their creators. Paul Reed Smith's McCarty Soapbar solid (pages 142-143) is a tribute to the former Gibson President, who has acted as a consultant for PRS; and we conclude by featuring Jerry Jones' superb revival of Nathan Daniel's 1960s sitar guitar alongside a striking modern reworking of the century-old "harp guitar" concept by another leading contemporary luthier, Steve Klein.

Steinberger solid-body, with "American Flag" artwork by Jan Lawrence, 1997. U.S. designer Ned Steinberger pioneered the concept of "headless" guitars; the tuners on instruments like this one are located on the bottom edge of the bridge/tailpiece.

(Courtesy Rod & Hank's, Memphis)

CHAPTER 6
TOWARDS THE FUTURE

*I*t is now three decades since Alembic co-founder Ron Wickersham fitted custom electronics into instruments owned by two leading San Francisco Bay area musicians – Grateful Dead bassist Phil Lesh, and singer/songwriter/guitarist David Crosby (who still uses the Guild twelve-string containing his original Alembic pickup). Since then, some of the approaches Ron pioneered have become standard practice among guitar and electronics designers; but back in the late 1960s, many performers were still struggling to find high performance equipment that could stand up to the rigors of rock playing. As his daughter Mica (now Alembic's General Manager) explains, "Probably the main driving force to make the instruments the way they were was the musicians themselves. Jack Casady [of Jefferson Airplane], Phil Lesh and David Crosby were very articulate at describing their frustrations, and my dad is a very good listener; so he could understand exactly what the problems were and help to solve them."

When guitarists and bass players came to Ron Wickersham wanting lower noise levels, increased dynamic range and wider tonal variation from their instruments, he was able to answer their needs using the skills he had developed as a broadcast engineer. Unlike some technical experts, who, in his words, regarded rock as "a fad – something people wouldn't need good tools for," he loved the music, appreciated the problems posed by powerful amplification and high volume playing, and sought to give musicians the freedom to create the sound they wanted. "When you did provide a tool with more versatility, then more music came out, and people discovered the music that may have been trapped in their heads – [music that] they didn't even know they were having trouble getting out!"

Alembic's current instruments, like its earliest ones, aim to offer the widest possible range of tone-colors and to minimize noise and interference through the use of low impedance circuitry, active pre-amps, and specially designed pickups with ceramic magnets. Two fine recent models are illustrated here: the California Special, whose six-in-line headstock and distinctively shaped body are new departures for the company; and the six-string Orion bass – a set neck instrument also available as a four- or five-string.

Above and right: *Alembic California Special, 1998. This instrument retains the neck-through-body construction found on most Alembics, but its solid maple body and slightly Strat-like overall shape are, in the words of the company's publicity, "perfect for those situations where the 'hippie sandwich' look might not be appropriate." ("Hippie sandwich" is an affectionate and widely used nickname for "traditional" Alembic bodies like those illustrated in Chapter 4, which are built up from several layers of wood.) The California Special is fitted with two single-coil pickups in the neck and middle positions, and a humbucker at the bridge. Alembic staffer Eric Coleman created the custom finish on this example.*

Left: *Alembic Orion six-string bass, 1998. The Orion is based on Alembic's popular Europa model, but has a set neck of cross-grained maple instead of the Europa's neck-through-body design. Its body has a mahogany core, and is available with a wide range of top laminates; the fingerboard is ebony. It is fitted with two Alembic MXY56 pickups, and has controls for volume, pan (blend between the pickups), and treble and bass.*

Guitars by Paul Reed Smith
and Ken Parker

Rock and jazz are radical forms of music, but the guitarists who play them often have strongly conservative views about instrument design. After more than 40 years, the classic Fender and Gibson solid-bodies are as popular as ever, and many musicians still believe them to be unsurpassed in terms of sound and feel. Significantly, a number of successful contemporary guitar makers share their customers' reverence for the past, and seek to develop, perfect, and even combine key aspects of the old "favorites" in their current models.

Maryland-based luthier Paul Reed Smith has used this approach brilliantly. His guitars are elegant, versatile, and full of new ideas, while incorporating two familiar basic features: a Gibson Les Paul-style carved top and glued-in neck, and a Strat-like double cutaway and vibrato unit. Reed Smith's designs have evolved through years of experimentation and "field-testing" in live performance. As a struggling young craftsman in Annapolis, he would obtain backstage passes to concert venues and offer his instruments to star players on the understanding that "if [they] didn't love the guitars they didn't have to pay me even when I knew I couldn't make my rent the

Below: *Paul Reed Smith Custom 22, 1997.*

(COURTESY CHANDLER GUITARS, KEW)

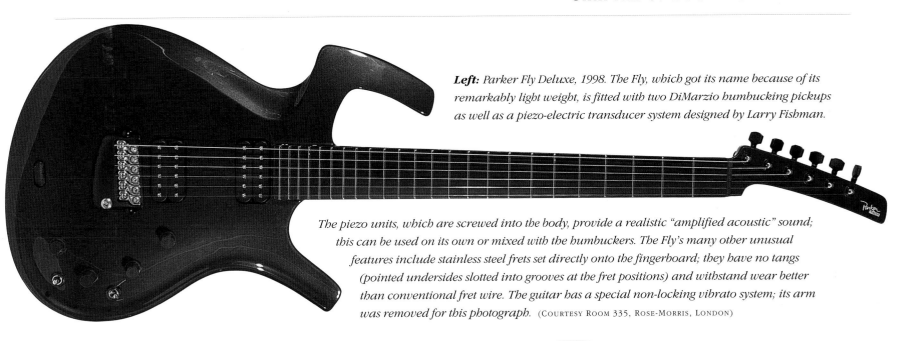

Left: *Parker Fly Deluxe, 1998. The Fly, which got its name because of its remarkably light weight, is fitted with two DiMarzio humbucking pickups as well as a piezo-electric transducer system designed by Larry Fishman.*

The piezo units, which are screwed into the body, provide a realistic "amplified acoustic" sound; this can be used on its own or mixed with the humbuckers. The Fly's many other unusual features include stainless steel frets set directly onto the fingerboard; they have no tangs (pointed undersides slotted into grooves at the fret positions) and withstand wear better than conventional fret wire. The guitar has a special non-locking vibrato system; its arm was removed for this photograph. (COURTESY ROOM 335, ROSE-MORRIS, LONDON)

Right: *Paul Reed Smith McCarty Soapbar, 1998. This instrument pays homage to Ted McCarty, the former President of Gibson, who was responsible for the introduction of the Les Paul and many other classic designs. Its pickups are modern re-creations (built by Seymour Duncan) of Gibson's vintage single-coil P-90 "soapbar" unit. The guitar has a solid mahogany body and a rosewood fingerboard.* (COURTESY ROOM 335, ROSE-MORRIS, LONDON)

Below: *The Paul Reed Smith Custom range was launched in 1985; this 22-fret model (24-fret necks are also available) has a carved maple top, a mahogany back and neck, and a rosewood fingerboard. Its pickups are PRS Dragon I humbuckers. The instrument is fitted with three control knobs: a conventional volume and tone, plus a rotary selector switch offering five different pickup configurations (including coil-taps and series/parallel switching).*

The guitar's tremolo arm was removed for this photograph.

next day." His efforts eventually paid off, and today PRS guitars, which are favorites of Carlos Santana and many other famous names, are in demand all over the world.

At first sight, there is absolutely nothing traditional or orthodox about the work of another leading American luthier, Ken Parker, whose Fly Deluxe is illustrated above. But beneath this instrument's carbon- and glass-fiber outer shell (or "exoskeleton") is a core of resonant wood, and Parker, who started out as an archtop maker, has likened his design to the construction of Renaissance lutes, whose sound was similarly enhanced by the use of softwoods covered in ebony veneers. The Fly is certainly an extremely responsive guitar, and its electronics – incorporating piezo-electric pickups as well as humbuckers – offer the player a wide palette of "acoustic" and electric tones. It is also remarkably comfortable and well balanced, and weighs less than 5lb (2.3kg). Since its introduction in 1993, it has attracted a number of high-profile users, including David Bowie's guitarist Reeves Gabrels.

Hugh Manson's Multi-necked Guitars

For many rock listeners, the use of double-neck guitars conjures up images of the progressive and jazz-rock scenes of the 1970s, with stars such as Jimmy Page and John McLaughlin reaching new heights of virtuosity on their Gibson double-necks – which combined standard six strings with twelve-string or bass necks and pickups. Multi-neck lap steels had been a familiar sight since the 1930s, but according to guitar expert George Gruhn, the first electric, double-neck Spanish-style instruments began to appear in the late 1950s, when Gibson produced a hollow-body six- and twelve-string (the EDS-1275) as well as a double-neck mandolin. These models were available only to special order, and in about 1962 they were joined by a bass- and six-string, SG-style guitar, the EBSF-1250.

Perhaps instruments like these were a little ahead of their time; it took the first stirrings of progressive rock to establish them fully. By the 1970s, with this musical movement in full swing (and the 1275 temporarily discontinued by Gibson), their popularity had grown considerably, and cheap double-neck copies had begun to emerge from the Far East. Meanwhile, at the other end of the price and quality scale, a number of famous players were commissioning individual luthiers to produce double- and multi-necked guitars to their own exacting specifications.

Hugh Manson, of Sandford, Devon, is undoubtedly the UK's leading maker of electric guitars of this type. His brother Andy, also a distinguished luthier, specializes in unusual acoustic instruments; their customers include John Paul Jones of Led Zeppelin, who, when asked about what he spent most of his money on during a recent survey, replied, "Buying guitars from Hugh and Andy Manson." Another of Hugh's regular clients, a leading rock guitarist, was so eager to see the blueprints for his new Manson guitar that the plans for it had to be redrawn to fit into the fax machine!

As Hugh explained earlier in this book (see pages 124-125), he enjoys the challenge of designing and building wholly original instruments; and the three examples of his work shown here, all commissioned by musician Paul Evans, clearly demonstrate his ability to create guitars that are musically and aesthetically unique.

Right: Hugh Manson custom double-neck, c.1996 This model is a combined six-string guitar and six-string bass. It has a maple body and an ebony fingerboard, and is fitted with EMG pickups. Both necks are headless; the standard guitar section incorporates a vibrato and a locking nut. The instrument's strings are tuned using the adjusters on each tailpiece.

(COURTESY PAUL EVANS)

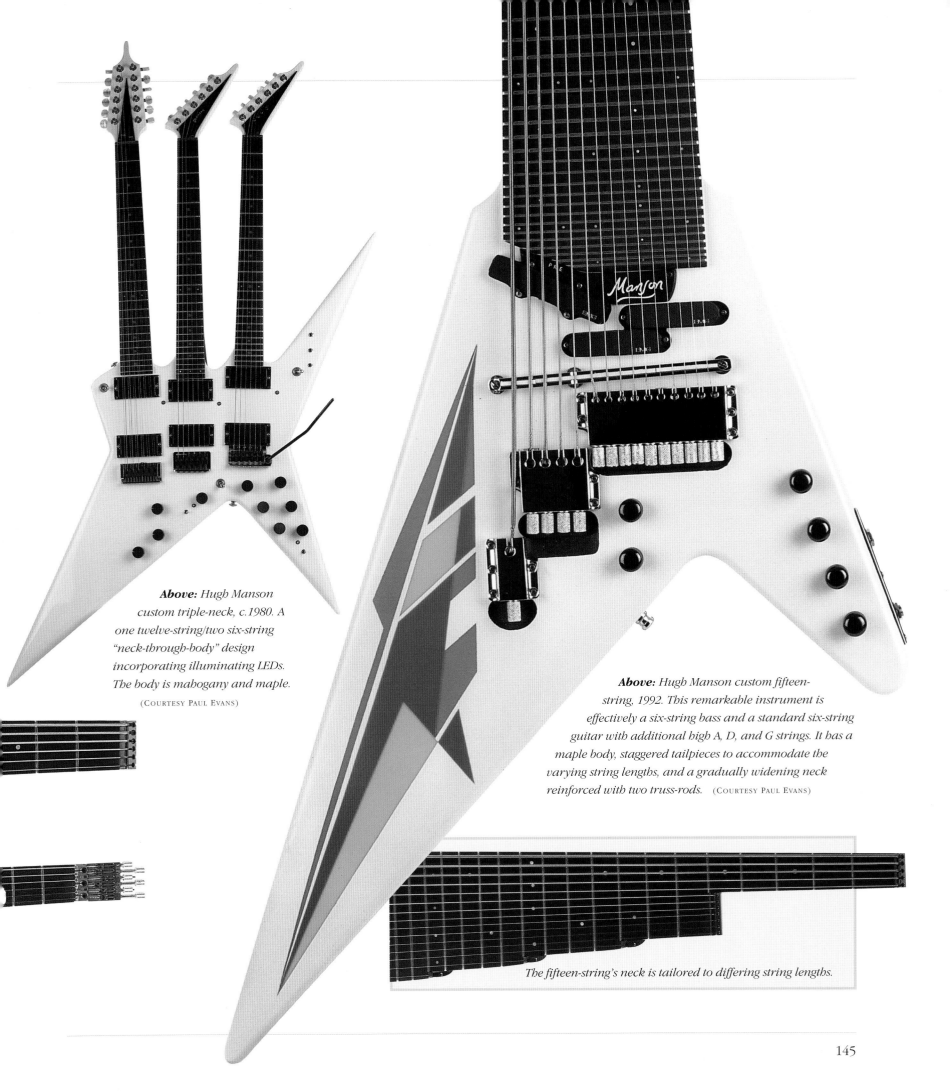

Above: *Hugh Manson custom triple-neck, c.1980. A one twelve-string/two six-string "neck-through-body" design incorporating illuminating LEDs. The body is mahogany and maple.*
(COURTESY PAUL EVANS)

Above: *Hugh Manson custom fifteen-string, 1992. This remarkable instrument is effectively a six-string bass and a standard six-string guitar with additional high A, D, and G strings. It has a maple body, staggered tailpieces to accommodate the varying string lengths, and a gradually widening neck reinforced with two truss-rods.* (COURTESY PAUL EVANS)

The fifteen-string's neck is tailored to differing string lengths.

Emmett Chapman
and The "Stick"

The Stick® is an ingenious and versatile electric stringed instrument with a substantial, steadily widening base of players throughout the world. Its inventor, Emmett Chapman, started out as a jazz guitarist; in 1964, while stationed with the U.S. Air Force in Omaha, Nebraska, he built himself a nine-string electric, and used it to develop his own highly original fingering techniques. As he explains, "I was playing complex chords in the style of jazz pianists while trying to free my melody lines in the style of Jimi Hendrix. Under Hendrix's influence I had the urge to play standing up, sliding my left hand around on the fingerboard, and doing one handed hammer-ons and hammer-offs in his style." Hammering – making a string sound by pressing it firmly onto the fingerboard instead of picking it – is normally executed by the player's left (fretting) hand. However, during a practice session on August 16, 1969, Emmett repositioned his right hand perpendicular to the fingerboard (see photo), and began using both hands to hammer on and sometimes hammer off. This breakthrough revolutionized his playing style: "I threw out ten years of jazz guitar playing and started over".

Using Emmett Chapman's basic "two-handed tapping," players can, in his words, "do the common scalar fingering techniques with both hands equally, either independently or interdependently," combining chords and melodies in a rich, varied range of textures. Emmett modified his own guitar to take full advantage of these possibilities, changing its tuning, lowering the action, raising the pickups, incorporating a string damper, and creating a double strap system to position the instrument more vertically. In 1970, he built a bodiless version of the newly evolved instrument out of an ebony board, naming it "The Electric Stick." This ten-string model went into commercial production four years later, and Emmett and his staff now produce about 50 instruments at a time over two and three month periods from their headquarters in Woodland Hills near Los Angeles. These include the original standard Stick and the twelve-string Grand Stick® introduced in 1990 (each encompassing a range of over five octaves), as well as their newest model, an eight-string Stick Bass®.

Emmett Chapman

Above and opposite page, inset: Chapman Grand Stick, 1998. This model is made from laminated cherry wood; a variety of other timbers, including rosewood, teak, oak and some African hardwoods are also available. Unlike many electric guitars, whose fingerboards are designed to have a slight camber, the Stick's playing surface is absolutely flat. Its frets are stainless steel rods, slid into place from the side of the neck; these are far more durable than conventional fret wire, and are round and smooth to the fingers. The strings are divided into two groups – melody and bass – with the lowest pitched strings placed in the center. Each string's height, length, and position can be adjusted via the bridge and tailpiece assembly. The Block™ pickup module contains two active, humbucking transducers, and allows signals from the two string groups to be processed separately in stereo, or combined in mono.

Below right: Chapman prototype, 1964. Emmett Chapman's uniquely designed guitar, which led to the discovery of two-handed tapping, was built in the woodshop at the USAF base in Omaha, Nebraska, where he was stationed. Emmett's first attempt at instrument-making, it began with nine strings, but later underwent extensive modification to enable the "Stick" tapping method. It is a neck-through-body design, with a center section of maple; the pickup assembly has been removed, but the bridge, jack-socket, and one of the controls are still in place.

Right: "The Block" – the pickup housing is mounted on rubber-tipped set screws to isolate it from the body.

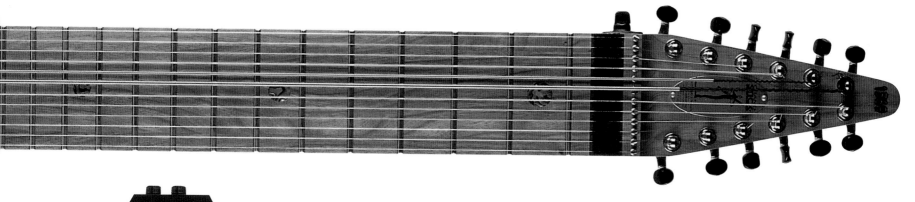

Above: *Chapman Stick Bass, 1998. Unlike the Standard and Grand Sticks, the Stick Bass has a more conventional "top-to-bottom" tuning system; its eight strings are pitched in fourths, with the lowest (B) string corresponding to the note a fourth below the bottom string of a standard bass guitar. (The instrument can also be configured for other tunings.) Its neck and overall dimensions are the same as the standard ten-string Stick, but with wider spaced strings. It is fitted with active EMG pickups, switchable from stereo to mono.*

(ALL PHOTOGRAPHS ON THESE PAGES COURTESY EMMETT CHAPMAN)

The Old and The New

Acoustic "harp guitars", with up to twelve unfretted extra bass strings, were produced by a number of leading American companies, including Gibson, Martin, and the Larson Brothers (who marketed their harp guitars under the Dyer label) from the early 1900s onwards. The Dyer design, which had only five additional strings, proved to be the most manageable and successful of these instruments, and in the 1980s, the brilliant young American guitarist/composer Michael Hedges (1953–1997) regularly played a 1920s Dyer model onstage and in the studio. A little later, Hedges switched to a new, electric harp guitar specially made for him by Californian luthier Steve Klein. This was fitted with two EMG pickups, and also had a Steinberger "TransTrem" bridge – a highly sophisticated transposing tremolo unit that allows the player to lock the six main strings into higher or lower tunings with its controlling arm. The Klein harp guitar shown opposite is almost identical to the one used by Hedges, but does not include the TransTrem.

National's Reso-lectric is another ingenious combination of old and new. It features a single resonator unit of the type first developed by John Dopyera (1893–1988), and subsequently used in a wide range of metal- and wooden-bodied instruments. The guitar has a Highlander piezo pickup mounted inside its "biscuit" bridge, providing a convincing electric version of the classic National resonator sound. Its output can be mixed with the signal from the magnetic "soapbar" pickup positioned near the neck. The Reso-lectric is also effective when played acoustically.

The final guitar shown here is a more direct rendition of an earlier design. During the mid-1960s, Nathan Daniel (see pages 50-51) responded to the vogue for Indian music in American and European rock circles, largely inspired by George Harrison of The Beatles, who at one time took sitar lessons from Ravi Shankar, by creating a "sitar guitar" with thirteen extra "drone" strings. Jerry Jones, whose fine replicas of other Daniel models are featured on pages 122-123, has now revived this remarkable instrument as well. It is currently attracting a number of adventurous players, many of whom are experimenting with custom drone tunings for special musical effects!

Below: *Steve Klein harp guitar, 1997. The instrument's basic body design is similar to Steve Klein's six-string electrics, but with a second headstock and supporting bars for the five additional strings. These have their own dedicated pickup (controlled by the volume knob beneath the five-string bridge); the "regular" guitar is fitted with two EMG humbuckers.*

(COURTESY KLEIN ELECTRIC GUITARS)

Below left: *Jerry Jones Electric Sitar, 1998. Like other Nathan Daniel designs, this guitar has "lipstick tube" single-coil pickups – two for the six main strings, and one for the thirteen drones, which are tuned chromatically in semitones. The extended, curved bridge is designed to enhance the "sitar-like" tone quality by buzzing slightly!*

Daniel's original instrument appeared under the Coral brandname; it was endorsed by guitarist and mandolinist Vincent Bell, who worked with Bob Dylan and a number of other leading players.

(COURTESY JERRY JONES GUITARS)

Below: *National Reso-lectric, 1997. The Reso-lectric has a single, 9¹/₂-inch (24cm) resonator cone recessed into its solid alder body. The Seymour Duncan P90 "soapbar" pickup and the Highlander piezo device installed in its bridge are switched and combined via two of the retro-style knobs on the upper bout; the third knob is a master volume control.*

(COURTESY NATIONAL RESO-PHONIC)

The instrument's top is made of maple veneer, and it has a hardrock maple neck and rosewood fingerboard.

Glossary

action Height of strings above the guitar's fingerboard. A low action makes it easy for a player to form notes and chords with his/her fretting hand, but may compromise the instrument's tone and cause string buzzing. High action often improves and boosts the sound, but can lead to playing difficulties.

active Guitars with active circuitry have volume and tone controls that offer an electronic boost ("gain") to the signals they process. Standard, *passive* guitar controls can provide only attenuation.

Alnico Type of magnet widely used in pickup manufacture. The name is derived from the magnet's constituent materials: aluminum, nickel, and cobalt.

archtop Guitar with *top* carved or pressed into an arched shape (cf *flat-top*).

back pickup Pickup mounted closest to the *bridge*, providing a cutting, treble-rich tone often favored for solo passages.

binding Strip(s) of wood, plastic, or other material decorating the edges of a guitar's body.

bout Most guitars have bodies shaped like a figure-of-eight; the wider sections above and below the *waist* are referred to as the upper and lower bouts. *Archtops* and *flat-tops* are frequently categorized by the maximum width of their lower bouts (17 inches/43.2 cm, 18 inches/45.7 cm, etc.)

bridge Unit mounted on the lower part of a guitar's *top*, and fitted with one or more *saddles* of metal, wood, or other materials. It sets the end of the strings' vibrating length (which begins at the *nut*), and can usually be adjusted to affect their height and intonation.

burl Naturally-occurring knot in a piece of wood.

carved top Arched guitar *top* shaped by hand or machine carving (cf *pressed top*).

CNC Computer Numeric Control. A method of controlling high precision machine tools with computers during guitar manufacture.

coil-tap Circuit that converts a *humbucking pickup* to *single-coil* operation.

combo, combo amp Amplifier and loudspeaker(s) combined in a single, portable unit.

cutaway Incision in the upper part of the guitar body adjacent to the neck, allowing the player's fretting hand to reach the highest positions more easily. See *Florentine cutaway, Venetian cutaway*.

decal Name tag or other symbol/trademark applied to an instrument via a transfer or similar means. Most often seen on guitar *headstocks*.

double-tracking Studio technique allowing an artist to overdub an additional part onto an audio recording s/he has already made.

drone string Unfretted string tuned to a preset pitch. Found on *harp guitars*, and on the sitar guitar illustrated on pages 148-149.

Electric Spanish Term used by Gibson (and some other manufacturers) for electric guitars designed to be played in the "traditional" position (i.e. held upright in the arms). The name (and the Gibson catalog prefix ES) differentiates these instruments from electric *Hawaiian guitars* (given the EH prefix by Gibson), which are placed horizontally on the performer's lap and fretted with a steel bar.

electro-magnetic pickup See *single-coil pickup, humbucker*.

feedback Howling or squealing effect caused when an electric instrument picks up its own amplified sound from a nearby loudspeaker. Some rock players deliberately induce feedback and use it as a musical tool.

flat-top guitar Steel-strung guitar with a flat (i.e. not arched) *top*.

floating pickup Pickup that makes no contact with a guitar's *top*, thereby preserving the instrument's acoustic integrity. (Pickups mounted directly onto the top tend to deaden its vibrations, compromising the acoustic sound.)

Florentine cutaway Term used by Gibson to describe the sharp-horned *cutaway* seen on guitars such as the ES-175 (pages 56-7). cf *Venetian cutaway*.

Frequensator Type of *tailpiece* designed by Epiphone and used on many of its *archtop* guitars from the late 1930s onwards. It has a double trapeze shape, and was intended to "equalize" treble and bass response by shortening the top three strings' path from bridge to tailpiece, and extending the length of the three lower strings. An example can be seen on pages 68-69.

fret Metal ridge inset across the fingerboard. Holding down a string behind a fret causes the string to be pressed against it, raising the pitch. Frets are positioned on the neck at intervals of a semitone.

front pickup Pickup mounted closest to the neck, providing a warm, rounded tone often favored for chordal and rhythm playing.

full-body, full-depth Hollow-body electric guitar with a body depth (typically c.3 inches/7.62cm) equivalent to that found on acoustic models.

harp-guitar Guitar with additional unfretted bass strings providing extended range. Developed by a number of late nineteenth/early twentieth century luthiers, notably Orville

Gibson (1856–1918), and revived, in a radically altered solid-body form, by Californian luthier Steve Klein (see pages 148-149).

Hawaiian guitar Guitar designed to be played in a horizontal position on the performer's lap. Notes and chords are formed using a metal bar instead of the fingers of the fretting hand, permitting the characteristic glissandi associated with Hawaiian guitar styles. The instrument's *action* is higher than a standard guitar's, and its neck profile is frequently square. Hawaiian guitars are also known as *lap steels*.

headstock Section of guitar neck above the *nut*. The *tuning machines* are mounted on it.

humbucker, humbucking pickup Twin-coil *electro-magnetic pickup* invented by Gibson engineer Seth Lover (1910–1997). Like the *single-coil pickup* from which it was developed, the unit is mounted under a guitar's strings. As these are struck, they create variations in the pickup's magnetic field and generate electrical currents in its double coils; the resultant signal is amplified and fed to loudspeakers. One of the humbucking pickup's coils is wired out-of-phase with the other; this has the effect of canceling or helping to suppress ("buck") hum and noise.

impedance Electrical resistance, measured in ohms. Nearly all standard guitars and their amplifiers are high-impedance, while most professional recording equipment uses low-impedance circuitry, which is less susceptible to noise, interference, and high frequency signal losses. The Gibson Les Paul Signature (see pages 88-89), and the Les Paul Personal and Recording models all incorporate low-impedance pickups.

jack socket Insertion point for the jack plug that connects an electric guitar to an amplifier.

laminate Material made by bonding together two or more thin sheets of different woods or other constituents.

lap steel Synonym for *Hawaiian guitar.*

locking nut Type of *nut* often fitted to guitars with advanced *vibrato units*. It features bolts or other devices to prevent strings going out of tune when the vibrato is used.

machine head See *tuning machine.*

Masonite Type of hardboard used in the construction of Danelectro guitars (see pages 50-51) and their replicas.

MIDI Musical Instrument Digital Interface – standard protocol for the exchange of performance data between synthesizers, sequencers, and other digitally controlled devices. Some specially equipped guitars can send and receive MIDI information.

neck-through-body Method of guitar construction in which a single piece of wood is used for the neck and the center section of the instrument's body.

nut Block of bone, ivory, ebony, metal, or synthetic material mounted at the *headstock* end of the neck. It sets the height and position of the strings as they pass through the grooved slots cut into it, and also acts like a *fret*, defining the start of the vibrating length of each open string (see *bridge*).

parallel Pickup coils are normally wired in "series" (i.e. with the same current flowing in turn through each of them). Some guitar makers equip their instruments with a switch to convert the pickups to "parallel," an electrical mode in which the same voltage is applied to each coil. This creates a thinner sound, somewhat similar to the effect of using a *coil-tap*, but with the advantage that a parallel-switched *humbucking pickup* retains its noise-reducing capacity, as both its coils are still in circuit.

passive Standard guitar volume and tone controls are passive (i.e. without *active* circuitry). They can reduce output level and attenuate higher frequencies, but are unable to boost signals from the instrument's pickups.

phase The electrical polarity of one pickup relative to another. Pickups on some guitars can be switched out-of-phase, creating a distinctive, slightly hollow-sounding tone.

pick See *plectrum.*

pickguard Protective plate of plastic, tortoiseshell, or other material, suspended (just below string height) above a guitar's *top*, or screwed directly onto its body. It is designed to protect the instrument's finish from damage by stray *plectrum* strokes.

piezo-electric pickup A transducer that converts vibrations from a guitar body or *bridge* into electrical currents which can then be amplified and fed to loudspeakers. Piezo-electric pickups provide a cleaner, more uncolored sound than electro-magnetic pickups (see *humbucker, single-coil pickup*).

plectrum Thin, pointed piece of plastic, tortoiseshell, or other material, held between the thumb and forefinger of a guitarist's striking hand and used to pick or strum the instrument's strings.

pressed top Arched guitar *top* pressed into shape (using heat or other means) instead of being carved out. (cf *carved top*).

purfling See *binding.*

Res-o-lectric unit Unit carrying a pickup and its associated wiring, designed by National in the 1930s to allow the firm's *resonator guitars* to be converted to electric operation.

resonator guitar Guitar originally developed by John Dopyera (1893–1988), fitted with one or more metal resonator assemblies. These instruments were manufactured by the National and Dobro companies, which merged in 1935.

reverse body Design where the instrument's treble wing or "horn" is larger/higher than the one on its opposite (bass) side.

saddle Platform made from wood, metal, or other material, mounted on (or forming part of) the *bridge* of the guitar at the point where the strings pass across it. Many electric guitar bridges feature individually adjustable saddles for each string.

scratchplate See *pickguard*.

semi-acoustic guitar A guitar fitted with one or more *electro-magnetic pickups*, but also featuring a hollow body and some degree of acoustic sound.

semi-solid guitar Guitar combining a solid construction (usually at its center) with hollow body cavities. The most famous example is probably the Gibson ES-335 (see pages 64-65).

series See *parallel*.

single-coil pickup *Electro-magnetic pickup* fitted with a single coil (as opposed to the *humbucker's* twin coils) and mounted beneath a guitar's strings. Their vibrations create variations in the pickup's magnetic field and generate electrical currents in the coil; these are amplified and fed to loudspeakers.

solid, solid body Electric guitar with no resonating cavities, constructed from a solid slab (or glued-together pieces) of wood.

soundhole(s) Hole(s), normally round, oval, or f-shaped, cut into a guitar's *top*. Their original purpose was to project the instrument's acoustic sound, but on many electric instruments their function is chiefly or exclusively decorative. Some Gretsch "Chet Atkins" models (see pages 74-75) have a sealed top (to reduce the risk of *feedback*) with faked, painted-on f-holes.

stop tailpiece, stud tailpiece Metal block-type *tailpiece* found on many *solid* and *semi-solid* electrics. Unlike the more traditional hinged trapeze tailpiece, the "stud" or "stop" unit is attached to the body only a little way below the *bridge*.

Superstrat *Solid* guitar with a shape roughly similar to the Fender Stratocaster, but fitted with more powerful pickups and *vibrato unit*, as well as other "hot-rodded" features.

tailpiece Metal or wooden fitting, installed below a guitar's *bridge*, and acting as an anchor for its string ends. Traditional *archtop* guitar-style tailpieces (also seen on some *solid-body* instruments), are often hinged and in a trapeze shape. Later, units such as the *stop* or *stud tailpiece* (qv) became popular with many makers and players.

thinline *Archtop* electric guitar with reduced depth (typically c. 1¾ inches/4.4cm) compared with its acoustic counterparts.

top The "face" of the guitar; its uppermost body surface, with pickups, *bridge* etc. mounted on it. The tops of *semi-acoustic* and many *semi-solid* instruments feature *soundholes* and bracing on their undersides.

tremolo arm, tremolo unit, "trem" See *vibrato unit*.

truss-rod Metal bar inserted into a guitar neck to improve its strength and rigidity. Most electric guitars have adjustable truss-rods whose tension can be changed to correct bowing or warping in the neck.

tuning machine Geared string-tuning mechanism mounted in the guitar's *headstock*.

Venetian cutaway Term used by Gibson to describe the rounded-horn *cutaway* seen on guitars such as the ES-5 (pages 58-59). cf *Florentine cutaway*.

vibrato unit, vibrato arm
Mechanical device, usually attached to or built into a guitar's *tailpiece*, which allows the player to create pitch bends by loosening or tightening the instrument's strings with a lever or arm. Vibrato is the musical term for rapid pitch fluctuation, while *tremolo* is the effect produced by a series of fast repetitions of the same note. Therefore, "vibrato unit" is the correct name for pitch-bending devices of this kind, although many manufacturers and players refer to them as "tremolos" or "trems."

Vibrola Type of *vibrato unit* invented by Clayton O. ("Doc") Kauffman and used on many Rickenbacker guitars.

whammy bar Nickname (used by rock and especially heavy metal guitarists) for a *vibrato* or *tremolo* arm.

Wildwood Type of dyed wood produced in Scandinavia and used by Fender on some of its instruments (see pages 82-83).

X-bracing Method of strengthening the *tops* of guitars and controlling/modifying their tonal characteristics by using struts crossed in an "X" pattern. It was first popularized by C.F. Martin (1786–1873), and has become a standard method of bracing for *flat-top* and some *archtop* designs.

Bibliography and Discography

Achard, Ken: *The History and Development of the American Guitar*, Musical New Services Ltd., 1979

Bacon, Tony: *The Ultimate Guitar Book*, Dorling Kindersley, 1991

Bacon, Tony & Day, Paul: *The Gretsch Book*, Balafon, 1996

Bechtoldt, Paul, & Tulloch, Doug: *Guitars from Neptune – A Definitive Journey into Danelectro Mania*, Self-published, 1995

Benedetto, Robert: *Making an Archtop Guitar*, Centerstream, 1994

Brozman, Bob: *The History and Artistry of National Resonator Instruments*, Centerstream, 1993

Chinery, Scott & Bacon, Tony: *The Chinery Collection – 150 Years of American Guitars*, Balafon/Miller Freeman, 1996

Denyer, Ralph: *The Guitar Handbook*, Pan, 1982

Dobson, Richard: *A Dictionary of Electronic and Computer Music Technology*, Oxford University Press, 1992

Duchossoir, A.R.: *The Fender Stratocaster (40th anniversary edition)*, Hal Leonard, 1994

Duchossoir, A.R.: *The Fender Telecaster*, Hal Leonard, 1991

Duchossoir, A.R.: *Gibson Electrics – The Classic Years*, Hal Leonard, 1994

Evans, Tom and Mary Anne: *Guitars from the Renaissance to Rock*, Oxford University Press, 1977

Freeth, Nick & Alexander, Charles: *The Acoustic Guitar*, Courage Books, 1999

Gruhn, George & Carter, Walter: *Electric Guitars & Basses – A Photographic History*, Miller Freeman Books, 1994

Gruhn, George & Carter, Walter: *Gruhn's Guide to Vintage Guitars*, GPI Books, 1991

Grunfeld, Frederic V.: *The Art and Times of the Guitar*, Da Capo, 1974

Hounsome, Terry: *New Rock Record (third edition)*, Blandford Press, 1987

Jasper, Tony & Oliver, Derek: *The International Encyclopedia of Hard Rock & Heavy Metal*, Sidgwick & Jackson, 1983

Kernfeld, Barry (ed.): *The New Grove Dictionary of Jazz*, Macmillan, 1988

Longworth, Mike: *Martin Guitars, A History*, 4 Maples Press Inc., 1988

Malone, Bill C.: *Country Music, U.S.A. (revised edition)*, University of Texas Press, 1985

Moseley, Willie G.: *Stellas & Stratocasters – An Anthology of Articles, Interviews, and Columns from the Pages of Vintage Guitar Magazine*, Vintage Guitar Books, 1994

Obrecht, Jas (ed.): *Blues Guitar – The Men Who Made the Music*, Miller Freeman/GPI Books, 1993

Priestley, Brian: *Jazz on Record – A History*, Elm Tree Books, 1988

Smith, Richard R.: *Fender: The Sound Heard 'Round the World*, Garfish Publishing Company, 1996

Smith, Richard R.: *The Complete History of Rickenbacker Guitars*, Centerstream, 1987

Stimpson, Michael (ed.): *The Guitar – A Guide for Students and Teachers*, Oxford University Press, 1988

Summerfield, Maurice J.: *The Jazz Guitar (third edition)*, Ashley Mark, 1993

Trynka, Paul (ed.): *The Electric Guitar*, Virgin, 1993

Various: *The Gibson*, Rittor Music Europe Ltd./ International Music Publications Ltd., 1996

Wheeler, Tom: *American Guitars – An Illustrated History*, Harper-Collins, 1990

White, Forrest: *Fender: The Inside Story*, GPI Books/Miller Freeman Books, 1994

DISCOGRAPHY

Section One: The Birth of the Electric Guitar

Chapter 1: The Early Years 1930–1945

Important early Electro/Rickenbacker players (see pages 16-17, 22-23) included the virtuoso Hawaiian guitarist Sol Hoopii, whose work can be heard on *Hawaiian Steel Guitar Vols. 1 & 2* (Folklyric). Probably the most influential Rickenbacker player from the immediate post-war period was Jerry Byrd, who uses a Bakelite lap steel on Hank Williams' classic 1949 song, *I'm So Lonesome I Could Die* (*Alone and Forsaken*, Polydor).

Charlie Christian (pages 20-21) was chiefly responsible for introducing the electric guitar to jazz; several of his recordings with the Benny Goodman Orchestra have been reissued on *The Genius of the Electric Guitar* (CBS). Christian's advocacy of the electric guitar inspired many other players to take up the instrument; one musician, Mary Osborne, heard him playing with the Alphonso Trent Band in 1938, and went out the next day to buy herself a Gibson electric (probably an ES-150). Osborne later had a successful career on the New York jazz scene; a CD anthology of her work, *Mary Osborne: A Memorial*, is on the Stash label.

Section Two: The Classic Designs

Chapter 2: The Solid-Body Electric 1946–1965

Fender Telecaster (pages 30-33; also 78-79):
In the pre-rock and roll years, Leo Fender's main

customers were country players: one major name who promoted the Telecaster was Jimmy Bryant, whose duo LP with steel player Speedy West, *2 Guitars Country Style* (Capitol, out of print) is well worth tracking down.

Some Telecaster-playing country artists, like James Burton, soon gained wider recognition in mainstream pop. Burton worked for several years with Ricky Nelson, and later joined Elvis Presley's backing band, appearing on many of Presley's recordings from 1969 onwards. Subsequently, he and other ex-Presley sidemen were featured on Gram Parsons' and Emmylou Harris' *GP* and *Grievous Angel* (Reprise). After Parsons' death, Burton continued to record and tour with Emmylou as a member of her Hot Band (*Profile/Best of Emmylou Harris*, Warner Bros., 1978).

The Telecaster was a vital ingredient in the music produced by the Stax record company in Memphis, Tennessee. The label's "house band" was Booker T. and the MGs, with Steve Cropper on guitar. His Tele can be heard on tracks like the MGs' own *Green Onions (The Best of Booker T and the MGs*, Atlantic) and Otis Redding's *(Sittin' On) The Dock of the Bay (Otis Redding – The Definitive Collection*, Atlantic).

Fender Stratocaster (pages 34-37; also 80-81, 108-109): Buddy Holly was the first major pop artist to adopt the Stratocaster, and his worldwide fame ensured that the instrument was seen, heard, admired and desired by young guitarists everywhere. Most of Holly's classic songs can be found on *20 Golden Greats* and *Love Songs* (both MCA).

Among the early British users of the Strat (at a time when the instrument was hard to obtain outside America) was Hank Marvin of The Shadows; his career is documented on *The Very Best of the Shadows* (MFP).

Many of the blues-influenced British guitarists who emerged in the 1960s were also Stratocaster devotees. The Yardbirds included Strat-user Jeff Beck (who had replaced Eric Clapton – later to be strongly associated with Strats, but still preferring Gibsons at this stage in his career). The band's early albums with Clapton include *Five Live Yardbirds*, and *The Yardbirds* (Charly); Beck can be heard on *Roger the Engineer* (Edsel).

Jimi Hendrix was probably the most innovative of all Strat players; his classic LPs include *Are You Experienced?* and *Electric Ladyland* (both Polydor).

In the 1970s, Eric Clapton became a dominating force in the realm of Strat-playing, having previously been a Gibson user. Polydor's 2 CD set *Backtrackin'* features his work with Cream, Derek and the Dominoes, and tracks from his subsequent solo albums.

Another Strat lover, who also plays Pensa and Schecter solids (see pages 110-111, 134-135), is Mark Knopfler. Among his classic albums with Dire Straits are *Dire Straits*, *Communique* and *Love Over Gold* (Vertigo); his solo/duo albums include *Neck and Neck* with Chet Atkins (Sony) and *Golden Heart* (Warner Bros.)

Gibson Les Paul (pages 38-43; also 88-89, 104-105): Les Paul's solo records, and his duets with Mary Ford, can be heard on *The Legend and the Legacy* (Capitol, 4-CD set). After the Les Paul had been redesigned and then temporarily discontinued in favor of the SG, older models were favored by British players such as Eric Clapton (see above); Jimmy Page, subsequently lead guitarist with Led Zeppelin (*Led Zeppelin – Led Zeppelin IV*, Atlantic); and Peter Green, a member of the first incarnation of Fleetwood Mac (*Mr. Wonderful*, Blue Horizon, and *Then Play On*, Reprise). By the 1970s, the Les Paul became almost ubiquitous in progressive rock circles, and its many gifted exponents included Paul Kossoff of Free (*Free* and *Fire and Water*, Island); and Joe Perry of Aerosmith (*Toys in the Attic* and *Rocks*, Columbia).

Gibson SG (pages 42-45): The SG's devotees included the late Frank Zappa; a cross-section of his solos is featured on *Shut Up 'n Play Yer Guitar* (Columbia). The instrument has also appealed to Angus Young of AC/DC (*Highway to Hell*, EMI/Albert; *Back in Black*, EMI) and Black Sabbath's Tony Iommi (*Paranoid*, Vertigo).

Other solid-bodies: Elvis Costello played a Fender Jazzmaster (pages 46-47) on most of his early recordings for the Stiff label (including the albums *My Aim Is True* and *This Year's Model*).

Toots Thielemans can be heard with his Rickenbacker "Tulip" (pages 52-53) on the George Shearing Quintet's *Body and Soul* (A & M).

Gretsch's Duo-Jet (pages 52-53) has remained popular with several leading guitarists, including George Harrison, who used one (along with his Rickenbacker twelve-string and Gibson J160E electric Jumbo) on several early Beatles songs (*The Beatles – 1962–66*, Apple).

Chapter 3: The Hollow-Body and Semi-Solid Electric 1946–1965

The Gibson ES-175 (pages 56-57) has been used by many important jazzmen, such as Kenny Burrell (*Live at the Village Vanguard*, Charly Le Jazz) and Joe Pass (who also used a variety of other Gibson hollow-bodies–- a cross-section of his work is featured on the Pablo 4-CD set *Joe Pass – Guitar Virtuoso*). The ES-5 (pages 58-59) was also popular with a range of jazz and blues musicians; B.B.King is pictured playing one on the cover of his Ace compliation *Do the Boogie*. The Byrdland (pages 62-63), has become closely associated with hard rocker Ted Nugent (*Great Gonzos: The Best of Ted Nugent* – Epic). The ES-335's many devotees (see pages 64-65) include Larry Carlton (*Friends*, Warner Brothers); Lee Ritenour (*First Course*, Epic); and Bob Weir of the Grateful Dead (*Europe 72*, Warner Brothers). B.B. King used the 335 for a while, before switching to the ES-355 which he named "Lucille" (see pages 104-105). King's many fine albums include the all-time classic, *Live at the Regal* (MCA).

Chet Atkins has been a key proselytizer for Gretsch electric archtops (pages 72-75), and can be heard using them on the compilation *A Legendary Performer* (RCA), and more recently with Mark Knopfler on *Neck and Neck* (Sony). Gretsch were also favored by Eddie Cochran (*C'Mon Everybody*, EMI) and Duane Eddy (*The Best of Duane Eddy*, WEA). More left-field users of these classic instruments include "Poison" Ivy Rohrschach, guitarist with LA-based "psychobilly" combo The Cramps (*A Date With Elvis*, Big Beat).

Section Three: The Evolving Electric

Chapter 4: A Changing Climate 1965–1980 and Chapter 5: Innovation and Tradition – 1980 to the Present

Fender's semi-acoustic designs (pages 82-83) have never attained the popularity of their classic solid-bodies; however, British guitarist Dave Peabody can be heard using a Fender Coronado on the King Earl Boogie Band's recent CD *Feeling Good – Live in Denmark* (A New Day Records). Gibson's "Modernistic" guitars (pages 84-85) have a wider following: the Flying V's most famous user, bluesman Albert King, is featured on *The Masters* (Eagle), and *Wednesday Night in San Francisco* and *Thursday Night in San Francisco* (Stax). Andy Powell of British hard rockers Wishbone Ash is another Flying V devotee: Powerbright Records has produced a three volume *Archive Series* showcasing the band's back catalog.

The highest profile user of Alembic instruments (pages 90-93, 140-141) is bassist Stanley Clarke (*If This Bass Could Only Talk*, Sony). Alembic guitars have been favored by many West Coast rock bands since the 1970s; the musician who commissioned the Alembic seen on

page 91, John "Marmaduke" Dawson, was a member of the New Riders of the Purple Sage, whose eponymous debut album, and later LPs *Powerglide* and *Home Home On the Road* (Columbia) all feature guest appearances by Jerry Garcia and other members of the Grateful Dead.

The distinctive sound of Roger McGuinn's Rickenbacker twelve-string (pages 92-93) can be heard on The Byrds' *Super Hits* compilation (Columbia/Legacy). McGuinn has also recorded a number of excellent recent solo albums, including *Back From Rio* (BMG/Arista). Kurt Cobain's Fender "Jag-Stang" (pages 110-111) can be heard on his later recordings with Nirvana; a useful compilation of the band's work is *From The Muddy Banks of the Wishkah* (Geffen).

Jackson guitars (pages 112-115) can be heard on a considerable number of hard rock and heavy metal albums, including *Van Halen 1* and *2* (WEA), Ozzy Osbourne's *Blizzard of Oz* and *Diary of a Madman*, featuring Randy Rhoads on guitar (Jet), and Megadeth's *Cryptic Writings* (Capitol).

Steve Klein guitars (pages 116-117) are the choice of many leading players, including Bill Frisell, whose Klein electric is showcased on his album *Nashville* (Nonesuch).

Rick Turner's high-profile customers include Lindsey Buckingham (see pages 118-121) who has used Turner guitars on a range of Fleetwood Mac and solo projects since 1979. Rick has also recently made a guitar for leading avant-garde player Henry Kaiser to take to Antarctica for the continent's first-ever recording project.

The seven-string Robert Benedetto archtop shown on pages 130-131 has been used by its owner, Jimmy Bruno, on a number of recordings for the Concord Jazz label, including *Like That* (which features the guitar on its album cover); *Live at Birdland*; *Full Circle* (on which Jimmy duets with fellow-guitarist Howard Alden, Howard and Jimmy co-wrote the lead tune, *Benedetto Blues*); and *Live at Birdland II*.

Section Four: Today and Tomorrow

Emmett Chapman's Stick (pages 146-147) can be heard played by its creator on *Parallel Galaxy* (Back Yard Records). Other leading Stick performers include Tony Levin (whose contribution to King Crimson's 1981 album *Discipline* (EG) introduced many listeners to the instrument), and Trey Gunn (a member, with Levin, of the current King Crimson line-up). Gunn's latest solo album, *One Thousand Years*, is available on Discipline Records.

Index

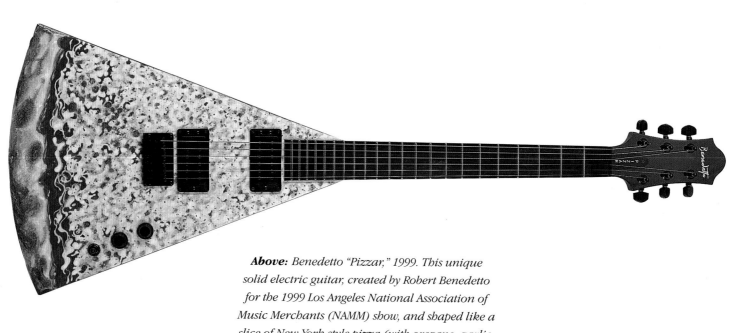

Above: *Benedetto "Pizzar," 1999. This unique solid electric guitar, created by Robert Benedetto for the 1999 Los Angeles National Association of Music Merchants (NAMM) show, and shaped like a slice of New York-style pizza (with oregano, garlic, and other herbs and spices sealed into its finish) was recently sold at auction in the U.S. Bob has no plans to make another "Pizzar," but will be producing some more "Unexpected Designs" in the near future!*
(COURTESY RICHARD GLICK, FINE GUITAR CONSULTANTS;
PHOTO BY JOHN BENDER, STROUDSBURG, PENNSYLVANIA)